Guesswork

Also by Martha Cooley

Thirty-Three Swoons
The Archivist

Guesswork

A Reckoning with Loss

Martha Cooley

Catapult   New York

Published by Catapult
catapult.co

ISBN: 978-1-936787-46-3

Catapult titles are distributed to the trade by
Publishers Group West
Phone: 800-788-3123

Library of Congress Control Number: 2016940497

Printed in the United States of America

9 8 7 6 5 4 3 2 1

In memory of my mother,
Nancy van den Hoek Cooley

Contents

Guesswork

1. The Stain

This morning, I finally visited *il cimitero.*

Before heading out, I scrubbed clean a half-dollar-sized, rust-colored stain I'd found on the bedspread in the guest room. The mark hadn't been there before breakfast, when I went to the room to retrieve something. While Antonio and I were eating, a cat must have entered the house and left us a souvenir of its presence. The fluffy-tailed cat, perhaps? Or maybe another, that black-and-white dandy who'd materialized on our terrace the other day, thin and tense. I'd given him a bit of prosciutto; he'd gobbled it and fled.

The stain was off the bedspread but not out of mind. Blood: as I rubbed the mark with a wet sponge, its color morphed from rust to red. Perhaps the cat was in heat. Or about to give birth? Meet death? I pulled the dampened cloth over the bed's footboard to dry, hearing in my head that darkly comic pair of lines from T. S. Eliot's *Sweeney Agonistes*: *Birth, and copulation, and death. / That's all the facts when you come to brass tacks.*

After a half hour of restless wandering about the house, I laced my shoes and, on impulse, ventured downhill.

I'd been avoiding *il cimitero* since our arrival in Castiglione del Terziere at the end of May, five weeks ago.

Not that there hasn't been much else to do. *Anzi*, as Italians say: quite the contrary. My husband and I have settled, more or less, into the house we've rented for the coming fourteen months, and have met our neighbors, including a few of the non-humans. (Yesterday, a yellow Lab called Pedro found me at the recycling bin and slobbered happily into my hand like an old pal.) We've taken several walks to nearby Croce and Pagazzana and explored what remains of the old footpath encircling the village of Castiglione. We've oriented ourselves, in other words. Gotten the lay of the land.

Except for the cemetery.

For me the quiet of the main macadam road, like the vacillating sun-shade-sun of its vistas, has served as a reassuring constant during our transition. The only sounds are those of crickets and birds; now and then, a low-pitched dance of water in the shallow stream below the goat pasture at the road's upper end.

As for the lane to *il cimitero*, I assumed it would be not only dark and solemn but very silent. It branched off the main road and descended swiftly. The sun broke through here and there, however, dappling the ground and revealing myriad spiderwebs in the undergrowth. And the sound that accompanied my footfalls was different from any I'd heard in the village: a low, steady hum. Not like that of a machine; not a radio on the fritz. I couldn't make out what was causing it until, right before the cemetery's gates, I saw a long row of wooden boxes, each on four legs. They extended the length of a sun-washed field whose grasses had been parched a dull buttery color by the summer heat.

Bees—an apiary, of all things! Right next to the town dead...

The bees were humming away; indeed, the noise increased as I proceeded. The music of industry, I thought. Of belief in *just do it*, in *getting ahead*, in *saving for a rainy day*. The song of collective labor, sweet production.

I pulled open the gates' heavy iron bolt, entered the dead's sanctum, and stared at the rows of headstones.

A half-dozen narrow concrete paths, each neatly edged with grass, separated the rows; by my rough count, there were fewer than fifty souls in the ground. Perhaps another fifty were interred in a high mortuary wall, behind which, out of sight, ranged the bees' boxes. Names and dates of birth and death were neatly carved on each of the headstones; some also bore photographs. Turning in a slow circle, I saw that the cemetery was full of color. Plastic bouquets of flowers, admirably realistic, stood erect or sprawled languidly across nearly every grave. At the rear, a whitewashed chapel presided over the group.

A cheerful cemetery, it seemed to me. With that hum all around, unremitting. Did the dead contribute to it? Did they spend all day adding their voices to the chorus, get their rest at night, and begin again at daylight?

Sun, hum, shade: a mix of tranquility and sprightliness. The dead here had a nice deal, with none of the lugubriousness or sententiousness of so many cemeteries. Their simple marble headstones were beautifully carved, unblemished by kitsch. A bit of birdsong provided the sole counterpoint to the bees. Then I heard a quick high wail, and a cat trotted toward me from one shady corner, tail aloft in greeting. It was a small tabby, its coat a mottled gold. As it approached, the cat slowed, then dropped gracefully to the ground and rolled over, exposing a pure-white belly. When it sat up again, whining delicately, I saw an exposed patch of skin behind one ear. Mites, mange, or a cat-fight had given the cat a bit of trouble recently; that circle of flesh wasn't suppurating, but it looked painfully raw.

I'll bring you something to eat next time, I told the cat. Now that I know you're here.

The cat took this as a benign signal, performed another rollover, and allowed my fingers to graze the very end of its tail as it slipped past me to a nearby patch of shade, which happened to be provided by Amelia Pizzi. Her tombstone was modest in size, unlike that of Liliana di Negro, who slept in a large berth in the wall, and whose name was inscribed in elegant cursive.

I wandered a bit, reading names and dates, supplying stories for the residents: this one might've died of that awful flu in 1918, this one could've been killed in World War II, that one must've been a kid in a car accident. Or with cancer. Or malaria. Or meningitis. Or—

They're not your dead, I said to myself as the stories, inadvertent and uninvited, began piling up in my head. You don't have to grieve for them, you don't know a soul here, it's not your job.

The cat atop the grave licked its front paws with serene thoroughness.

I have never been a visitor of cemeteries. Nor do I talk to my own dead. The idea of bringing them flowers has always seemed ludicrous to me. I don't ask them to intervene with anyone, human or divine, on my behalf.

The people who visit this place, I told myself (while the cat, finished with its ablutions, strolled back to its corner), are bringing flowers for themselves. Same goes for the conversations: when you talk to the dead, you're talking to yourself. When you cry, it's for yourself. You stage this whole drama— buying the flowers, dusting off the tombstone, offering the latest news of other family members, saying a fond farewell, stroking the headstone, promising to return soon—and you do it all for yourself. You say you're sad because they're not here to do it anymore, to *live*; but actually you're sad because you're still here, and there are things you wished you'd been able to ask or tell the dead and now you can't, and it seems terrible that all the unsaid, unasked stuff must back up in you like water in a pipe with no outlet, and you don't know how much

7

longer—a week, a year, many years?—you'll have to deal with that clog.

I started back to the main road. Along the lane, the hum was almost tactile, like a swath of velvet brushed lightly across my forehead, or the cat's fur on my fingertips. Bring a bit of food for that cat, I reminded myself. It'll be here for sure; you'll see it again. Assuming the injury behind its ear doesn't get infected and kill it. Or it doesn't die from a bee sting. Or get hit by a car on the road. Or—

As I walked home, I asked myself why I'd been reluctant to visit the cemetery. Why it seemed to require courage to do so, as if I'd be putting myself in some sort of danger.

I knew I wouldn't be. And in any case, terror of dying wasn't something I'd ever experienced, at least not consciously. For a long while I've cultivated an attitude of fatalism toward death. It would be different, surely, if I were dealing with a child mortally sick from the time of birth—or if, say, one of my beloveds were murdered before my eyes. But these aren't the norm; most of the time, people just get sick at some point, and die. And when people I've loved have died in an accident, or at a younger age than seemed right or fair, I've suffered but continued to believe death doesn't warrant agitation in advance. Jiggling an hourglass doesn't alter the sand's flow.

So why then my unease?

I realized, as I began panting on the uphill stretch of my walk, that a dream I'd had during my first week here, about

Andrea, my closest friend for over thirty years—a woman who died a few weeks after her forty-ninth birthday, of bowel cancer that metastasized to her liver—yes, it was that dream I'd had, unnerving in its perversity and coldness, which had served as the deterrent.

I'd evaded the cemetery because I'd feared reencountering not Andrea but the dream. In it—insofar as I could recall its details, for my psyche had done a good job of burying them— Andrea had insisted, in a tone of detached scorn, that I use my cock (in the dream, I had one) to enter her in her ass. She'd spoken as if she knew I had no idea what to do, no idea what she was talking about.

She was correct about my ignorance, as I didn't have a cock in real life, and I'd never thought about doing this to her while she was living. Sure, I'd thought about making love with her: what person, straight or gay or whatever, doesn't at some point think about making love with her best friend? For me, that time of thinking-about-it had occurred many years earlier, when we were on the cusp of thirty and took a trip to Haiti—a trip that was hot and difficult and entailed nights in sweltering rooms where we sat naked, swatting at insects and swilling beer and fanning ourselves, trying to cool down. But we hadn't had sex, or talked about having it. And that time had passed, and other things had happened in our lives; the eros of that moment had modulated into a different key. There'd been no subsequent moment or need to enact.

Our friendship went through tests over the next couple of decades, and was strengthened. Though we didn't live in the same city, for years we spoke on the phone several times a week. I saw Andrea regularly when I moved to her Brooklyn neighborhood in the late 1990s: we were one another's closest friends in the physical as well as emotional sense. When she died in 2005, the whole world seemed to go on tilt, and I wondered how it'd ever right itself.

Gradually, I learned to do my life without Andrea's companionship, to accept the things that had been hard about being her friend, to have my conflicts—of self, of memory—without her confirming or dissenting voice in my ear. To live my questions without hers as aid or distortion. To fall in love with someone she'd met once, but never got to know. To build a life in many ways different from the one she'd thought of as mine.

And then I came to Castiglione, and had a disturbing dream about her. And suppressed it. And thus didn't want to walk to the cemetery—which, as I walked back from it, was evidently meant to be the site of a necessary encounter. Not with Andrea herself (*she's dead, goddamn it!*), but with my missing of and longing for her, my relief that she was no longer present so I didn't have to account for myself with her, my sense that I'd outgrown her, my perplexity that I was older and that I had no idea what her life would've become—her marriage, her urge to draw and paint, her crippling self-doubt, her Buddhist practice, her body.

Her body, ravaged at the end yet so lovely at the start. Her feline sensuality. Her body, which never knew mine just as mine never knew hers. In my dream she'd asked of me something I couldn't give, wouldn't have wanted to . . . Was this yet another route my mind sought out of the morass of loss: setting her up as an aggressive interlocutor, asking of me something I couldn't give and wouldn't want to?

But why wouldn't I want to?

Well, of course. One day in the winter of 2001 she'd mentioned, in passing, a complaint, which she'd muttered in a mild tone, no panic—*I have blood in my stool* . . . The cancer was there, in that portal to her self, which, in the dream, she'd requested I enter. The request had been almost dismissive, as if to say, what do you *living* know? How can you understand what it's like to pass from health to death in so short a time? *The situation's getting rather dire*, she'd said to me near the end of her life, in a tone of gentle irony. Still, speaking about it slantwise is not the same as exploring, like Walt Whitman's solitary spider, *the vacant vast surrounding* while keenly aware that one's own filament will shortly give out. As Andrea knew, I would continue flinging my gossamer thread after her death. She and I were already following fundamentally different imperatives, though we hadn't yet parted.

Do it, said her gaze near the end—do it gladly, *musing, venturing, throwing, seeking . . . till the bridge you will need be form'd.* But do it by yourself now, without me.

A paradox: the words *together* and *alone* coexist in speech and feeling, yet logically cancel each other out.

The stain, I realized—that blotch on the bedspread— was the thing that brought all this forth. It was the stain that allowed me to confront my reluctance and visit the graveyard.

A little mark I'd tried to scrub clean, which, mercifully, claimed me nonetheless.

Tomorrow, I told myself, I'll bring some prosciutto to the tabby in *il cimitero*.

2. Sightings

Driving down the twisty macadam road to Villafranca one morning in late June, Antonio and I see two large black birds on an overhanging branch, beak to beak.

We slow down, stare. Their movements seem oddly stylized. They touch beaks lightly, tap-tap-tap, then make figure eights with their necks, pushing and nearly toppling each other. Then, disengaging, they hop around a bit, side by side, as if to warm up. Then touch beaks once more.

They're fighting, I think at first. Or wrestling.

Maybe kissing? Antonio proposes. Dancing?

Or feeding each other, I say. Or maybe arguing over food.

Staking a claim—isn't that how it's said, in English? Each bird claiming its right place?

But they keep hopping around, I answer. As if they don't know their right place.

Negotiating, says Antonio. Trial and error.

Dark feathers agleam in the sun, the birds continue their strangely purposeful dance, beak to beak. We stare a bit more, then turn to one another and shrug: we don't know what we're looking at. The guesswork is ours, not the birds'.

For the time being, I'm living in an in-between place: Lunigiana, a region in upper-central Italy unknown to most foreigners.

For the time being—a peculiar way of putting it. Why don't I just say Antonio and I are here *for now* rather than *for the time being*? The phrase seems to hint at a future when time might cease being, might devour its own entrails and leave not even a shred of itself to measure or consume. Is anything more voracious than time?

Sabbatical is the official term for this fourteen-month stretch of time away from home and work. Or *leave of absence*, as it's sometimes called. *Caesura* is my own word for it. In music and poetry, a caesura is a pause or break in a melodic line, a moment of in- or out-breath at a point of rhythmic division. In life—mine, anyway—it's a deliberate interruption, a chance to reckon with divisions imposed by loss. Multiple losses, actually: a friend, Lucy, to heroin ten years ago; Andrea to cancer three years later; and then, all in a row (or so it felt), six more friends to various illnesses—one, to suicide—in 2006, 2007, 2008, and 2010. Richard, Valeria, Liam, Nuala, Jason, David.

In the midst of this stretch my mother and father, both in their early eighties, had to be relocated to an assisted-living community. My father had begun showing early signs of dementia. My mother—who went gradually blind during my childhood, and has been sightless for the better part of four decades—had a heart attack. A bit later, she fell and broke her pelvis. Though she gradually returned to her usual state—lucid, wry, even-keeled—she can't walk more than a few feet, even with assistance. When I picture her now, I see her feet resting on her wheelchair's metal flippers and her hands in her lap, fidgeting ever so slightly.

In all this, I'm a fairly ordinary person. I haven't lost multiple family and friends to war, haven't had to reckon with the grim fact that *the numeral zero on the end / turns them into an abstraction*, as the poet Zbigniew Herbert put it. Thus far, the deaths that have touched me have all been civilian, and mostly a function of illness.

My father will be lost to me gradually, I expect, as his dementia increases. As for my mother, well, I've lost multiple versions of her over the years: the mother who would've seen my body become a woman's, the mother who would've gone traveling with me, the mother who would've turned her talents for weaving and ceramics into a genuine art practice, the mother who might've liked or might've disliked my choices of everything from skirts to men. (At the visual level, I mean. Which counts for plenty between mothers and daughters.) My mother and I never got to bicker over the color of my hair during the years I dyed it: is that a relief or a deprivation?

I'm four thousand miles from her now, in any case. She's delighted I'm on sabbatical, thinks it's marvelous for me—as indeed it is. Like my father, my mother has always encouraged travel abroad, and long separations from her children don't distress her. This lack of worry is a gift; I repay it by not focusing on the labored rasp I sometimes hear in her breathing when we speak by phone. She'd be vexed if she thought I was noticing. It's nothing, she'd say, I'm old, have you forgotten that? I reckon, too, that I can be at her side in less than a day, if need be. That's a calculation she's undoubtedly made as well, though she'd never mention it.

It's a good thing, this leave of absence: endorsed by parents, husband, friends, colleagues. And I tell myself I'm ready and able to take full advantage of it.

Yet I'm aware that's not entirely true, for my accumulated losses have upended me. The sand in my hourglass keeps dribbling, it doesn't reverse direction. But I've come through what's felt like a *strage*, a massacre; and while death appears to be taking a break (for the moment, anyway) from rat-tat-tatting my circle of family and friends, I'm still down in an emotional crouch, hands over head.

Admitting this makes me wince. After all, *I* haven't been gunned down; what am I complaining about? Yet despite the privileges of health, a happy marriage, and a gratifying job in academia, for the past ten years my life-work—my writing— has felt invalid, in both senses of that word: weak and spurious, feeble and unconvincing. The urge to *just do it* that used to counteract self-doubt won't buoy me. Each day, shame indicts me. Prior to their departures, none of my deceased friends ever made death the fall guy, nor did they whine about whatever they weren't accomplishing. I picture them conferring and agreeing: *too bad she can't wake up.*

Lunigiana is formally Tuscan, though its residents ignore the label. It's not Ligurian or Emilian, either; it belongs neither to the coast nor to the plain. An in-between place without its own dialect, Lunigiana is frequently traversed by Italians and tourists en route elsewhere, yet isn't often thought of as a destination in its own right.

We've landed here by chance. Antonio hails from Lombardy, in northern Italy; to him, Lunigiana was merely a name before we fixed upon it while seeking a vacation spot last summer. Our aim was to find a cheap rural rental about an hour from Parma, where Antonio's daughter, Paola, lives. A desultory search of Italian websites led to a mention of a medieval village in the Lunigianese hills—and thus, after a phone call, we found ourselves lodged in a one-bedroom apartment over the arched entrance to Castiglione del Terziere. The apartment's proprietors (I can still recall Antonio's bemused smile when, after getting off the phone, he informed me of this) were the inhabitants of the village's castle: Loris Jacopo Bononi and Raffaella Paoletti.

Our week-long stay in the *borgo* was memorably spiced by an impromptu tour of the castle and several long dialogues— monologues, actually—with *il professore* Bononi, whose unconventional background as a doctor-pharmacologist and poet fascinated us. When it came time, a half-year or so later, to choose a sabbatical roost, Antonio and I found ourselves in immediate if startled agreement: *Hey, let's go back there . . .*

Wedged between the Mediterranean coast to the west, central Tuscany to the south, and the Emilian plains to the north, Lunigiana is scored by mountains—the Appennini and Alpi Apuane—and their foothills. The Magra River's countless tributaries lace a landscape studded with medieval castles atop high hills; towers, walls, and parapets emerge, hide, then emerge again, veiled and revealed by copses of trees. An ancient pilgrims' route, the Via Francigena, meanders through Lunigiana—it's the medieval road from France to Rome, walked by the faithful for centuries. All year long, backpackers hike this trail, water bottles bobbing at their sides.

Lunigiana's loose web of actual and imaginative trails reflects my inner topography, now that I'm not home in Brooklyn, not around English-speaking people, and not on vacation. For a stretch of time, my days will be uncharted; mentally and physically, I'll wander as and where I wish. The prospect is at once tonic and terrifying.

The heavy iron door of our house opens with a long, old-fashioned iron key that rotates twice, loudly, just as we were told it would. When we first moved in, we chuckled each time we used it: heavy and ornate, it's right out of *The Addams Family*. Now the big key seems normal, and our American one flimsy.

We heard about this rental not from the house's owner, who spends most of his time abroad, but from *il professore*.

With three floors (the third a drafty mansard), the house is livable in a slapdash way. Now and then the plumbing wreaks havoc with our neighbor's cellar, dumping wastewater there. The kitchen is sparely outfitted; we make do with four smallish burners and a large toaster oven. The steep staircases of the house—open-planked, without risers or decent handrails—aren't exactly up to code, as we'd say in English. Yet the interior space is ample for our needs, and the terrace a pleasure: it gives onto a tree-filled valley, serene at all hours.

The day we moved in, I let Antonio enter our new home on his own; I was too nervous.

Wait, I told myself. Have a quick look around outside, get your bearings.

Scanning the alley, I saw that our house was flanked by several others, all of whose foundations dated from the Middle Ages. At the corner of the alley stood a once-grand villa. Its windows lacked panes; its second- and third-floor balconies were rusted. Someone had nailed slats of wood across its open entryway, which emitted a strong odor of cat pee.

As I would soon discover, the owners of this villa—numerous members of a large family—had failed for years to reach any accord on its future. It wasn't the only neglected or abandoned property in the village. Like most of the region's medieval *borghi*, Castiglione had emptied out after World War II; nearly all of its residents left to seek jobs. Many of the village's houses underwent their own journeys as well, from seldom used to decrepit to uninhabitable.

Eccoci, I thought, gazing at the shuttered houses adjacent to ours. Here we are . . . Though they weren't falling down, these places clearly hadn't been occupied for quite a while. How had we managed not to notice how deserted Castiglione was?

Come up, *amore*, called Antonio from inside. Look at the marvelous view from our bedroom!

Nearly two months have gone by since our arrival here. The sand in the hourglass seems to dribble unevenly: some days fast, other days scarcely at all.

I've given myself permission, for the first time in several decades, to spurn my ordinary routines. For the next twelve months I'm improvising, making up each day as it goes along. And since English isn't spoken much in Lunigiana, I'm relying on my Italian, which is decent but not fluent. The in-between-ness I feel is due in no small part to my straddling of languages. Talking with Italians other than my husband is the equivalent of riding a roller coaster. Whenever possible, I avoid phone conversations, which dilute both the pleasure and the meanings of speech. *Non ho capito*, I'm frequently forced to confess: I don't get what you've just said, I can't follow you . . . When linguistic inadequacy frustrates me, I remind myself that no one, not even a native speaker, achieves full fluency in any tongue. That prize can't be awarded: the only winner is language itself.

Face-to-face makes things easier. A great deal can be gleaned from gestures, expressions, tones. And from touch, of course; a hand on a forearm, say. When I want to get my mother's attention, or she mine, that's how we've always done it. Not with a shake or a tug; simply a hand alighting, perched as if on a bough, fingers tickling like feathers. In place of glances, we trade touches. A secret language, this one, and different from what I imagine "normal" mother-daughter speech to be.

It's been thus for decades. All my adult life, I've noted the veiled looks and heard the soft grunts and giggles, fraught with meaning, exchanged by my female friends and their mothers. Because my mother is sightless, we do it differently: we always begin with a name. *Mom*, I'll say, or *Mimi*, she'll start, and we'll each know we're in dialogue. Our conversations are peppered with exclamations and laughs, but they're mainly conducted with words. Clarity's our goal; we've trained ourselves to avoid misunderstandings. They happen, of course: we're a mother and a daughter, we misconstrue each other. That's built into the software. But we don't get into trouble by starting off on the wrong nonverbal foot. Ours is a different challenge. *Non ho capito*: I have certainly felt, countless times, that I don't understand my mother. *I don't get how you manage this blindness every day; I don't understand why we didn't talk about what it was like for you to go blind; I don't see how we might speak of it now.*

A few hundred feet further down the road to Villafranca, a half-dozen swallows career giddily across the sky. Antonio downshifts; our old car grunts in response.

So playful, Antonio says, pointing. And totally different from those other birds, the weird dancers we just saw . . . I guess swallows use another language.

Wing-speak, I say. Not beak-speak.

We are driving to town for bread, fruit, fish, and wine. It's near-evening; pale sunlight dapples a field to our right. Everything around us is readying for nightfall. I imagine hitching our groceries to the swallows' wings and having the bags flown up to our house, to be dropped off at dusk.

Our house—which isn't "ours" yet but has come to seem so, despite being as unlike our Brooklyn apartment as swallows are unlike blackbirds—sits midway along an alley that runs parallel to an extremely steep cobbled lane.

This lane ascends all the way to the arched entrance to the upper *borgo* and the gates of Castiglione's castle. Despite the fact that it serves as the village's main street, the lane is barely wide enough for the smallest Fiat. Most people walk up the hill to avoid scraping their cars' sides. Going up and especially down the lane by car scares me; I picture our old VW's brakes failing and the vehicle gaining speed, aimed headlong at stone. We usually forgo the drive and haul things in our arms or upon our backs. Our car stays down in *la colla*—the piazza at the foot of the lane, where the provincial road dead-ends.

"Going home" is thus a matter of climbing. In Brooklyn, too, we must ascend: our place is on the third floor of a brownstone, and there's no elevator. But since arriving here and hiking uphill daily, I've become a connoisseur of the natural and man-made materials underfoot or at hand. There are knobbly cobblestones; patches of lichen that turn slippery when wet; large flat slabs of stone covered by cement, whose color varies from grayish to puttyish; and retaining walls, particularly the mossy one of the castle's garden. Rising across the alley from our front door, it restrains the unkempt terraces looming above us.

The garden wall isn't straight, and it bulges outward here and there. It lies mostly in shade, its mottled surface mixing tones of gray, brown, and green. A rough staircase of sorts, with uneven risers and narrow steps, is hewn into one end of the wall; apart from that precarious entryway, the hillside garden can be accessed only from the castle's lower terrace. Untended for at least a decade, the garden is choked by undergrowth and weeds. Scraggly olive and fig trees stick out at weird angles from their steeply pitched perches; large stones dislodged from the terraces mar the rows' symmetry, like bowling balls gone astray. The woodshed's roof has caved in, hiding desiccated heaps of logs.

The garden violates my sense—acquired, no doubt, via childhood picture books—that a castle ought to boast a stylish, well-maintained theater for displaying its horticultural and arboreal holdings. Yet this *giardino* is beautiful in its own decrepit way, and full of sounds. After rainfall, its misshapen trees release exuberant tinklings of water onto our alley whenever birds settle on crooked branches. In the evening, returning from a trip to *la colla* with the trash, I can hear small animals (not urban rats, thankfully, but martens or squirrels) scuttling in the underbrush. And on certain moonless nights—especially if there's a bit of mist—an owl's eerie call from somewhere deep in the garden is an aural magic wand, able to freeze me in place.

* * *

In the lower part of the *borgo*, a cat has recently given birth. One of the two kittens (perhaps there were more, gone now) has infected eyes. Antonio and I pass it as we walk up the lane, grocery bags in hand.

The mother of the kitten with infected eyes stays near her offspring, though I've noticed she vanishes from time to time, leaving the vision-impaired kitten to lurch and mewl. It's as though the mother has begun a process of disengagement, accepting the fact that one of her brood is likely to go blind. I find this quietly hair-raising, no doubt because it's the obverse of the situation in which I grew up: with my mother slowly losing her sight to retinitis pigmentosa, a rare, untreatable eye disease, and myself gradually realizing what was going to happen. In my prepubescent narcissism, I sometimes felt more upset by the knowledge that sooner or later I'd never again be seen by my mother than by the fact that she'd no longer be seeing anyone or anything. For her the curtain was dropping, the lights dimming, and how would (no, *could*) the dramas of our lives play out if she wasn't watching, seeing?

The kitten reacts with fear as I pass. I can't tell if that's because for the kitten my image is distorted, or because I'm near its mother and the kitten doesn't want anyone too close to her. I must've sometimes felt that way, too, about my own mother, though I don't remember. I do recall days when I felt I was walking a tightrope. There was "normal" on one side and a Munch-scream world on the other, and I was balancing—or trying to—on the rope.

Antonio and I turn off the lane onto the alley, and hike up to the house. I enter first, grateful for the coolness conferred by stone. The walls of the house are a foot thick—a blessing in summer.

In the kitchen we put away the groceries as twilight fades to dark. Antonio switches on the outdoor light; moths dart upward. Stepping onto our terrace, I gaze at the hamlet of Croce, its few lights twinkling across the vale between us.

Oh, says Antonio, the wine, we forgot the white wine . . .

Tomorrow, I say. We'll make another run to Villafranca.

At least, says Antonio, we needn't go on donkey-back. Can you say that—donkey-back, like horseback?

He gives a little bray remarkably like that of one of the donkeys over in Croce. Then follows it with a light chuckle, purely his own.

I guess so, I say. Though I've never heard someone use that word, so I'm not sure it exists . . .

Once more I'm caught between languages, clumsy in one and uncertain about the other. As with the garden's trees, so with myself: no secure perch. Antonio's been let off the hook for a year; he's back on his own linguistic terra firma. Oh, he moaned recently, but what'll I do when I return to Brooklyn and find that my English has . . . what's the word? Back-something?

Backslid, I say.

Yeah. When that happens, I guess I'll just have to be like Sisyphus, and push the rock up the hill again.

Yep, I respond. *Esattamente.*

And then I wonder how to deal with the other conflict that occupies my mind. On some days I'm lured mesmerically to the rabbit hole of loss, and am forced to thrash around down there like trapped prey. On other days all the losses seem to recede like any object in a rearview mirror once the accelerator's been pressed, and I've no trouble keeping my foot on the pedal of the present. And no desire to stop and look back.

In Villafranca, cars routinely nudge halfway out of driveways or parking lots, then pause. It's hard to gauge the drivers' intentions. Approaching a partly launched car, I wonder whether I've been noted.

This, too, is a replay of earlier challenges, those of my youth and adolescence. I recall silently dodging my mother when, making her way across a room—hands outstretched, fingers alert for furniture—she'd unwittingly aim not for the door but at me. To prevent bumps and collisions, my siblings and father and I learned to accelerate and decelerate around her, and to call out soft warnings: *To your left, the armchair. Careful of the floor lamp.*

Since arriving here, I've learned to curse softly in Italian at indecisive or careless vehicles. Reacting to an especially bad instance, however—some driver pulling out fast while looking the other way, or blocking a crosswalk—I mouth off to myself in foul English. Saying the same things in Italian, silently or aloud, would seem a pale translation of my anger.

Which isn't really anger, I realize, so much as fear. Not terror, not panic; a low-grade fear, a chronic anxiety. I'm afraid of having to steer amidst obstacles, or between languages. Scared I'll fail to grasp what's really happening around or inside me—to pick up on truths spoken by others, or somehow shaken loose within me—and by the time I do, it'll be too late; I'll have missed something important.

Whenever I mention my linguistic distress to Antonio, he smiles and shrugs. What do you think I've been dealing with since I moved to the States to be with you? he asks me one morning. Welcome to the sort-of-bilingual club!

Oh, come on, your English is way better than my Italian, I say.

No it isn't, he responds. And in any case, the feeling you're talking about won't go away. It comes with the territory, isn't that how you put it?

Yep. Just have to grin and bear it, I suppose . . .

Now *that's* a nice expression, Antonio says. English is so economical—look what you can do with a few monosyllables!

He pronounces that last word the Italian way, *mono-SIL-a-be*, which charms me. Then he wraps his arms around me and squeezes hard.

Siamo fortunati, he murmurs, *we're lucky*, and I know what he's talking about; he needn't say another syllable. We've been married for only a few years, though we've known each other nearly a dozen. A death, that of his wife, Valeria—my close friend, one of my keenest losses during the *strage*—brought us unexpectedly together. She was my age, fifty-seven, when back pain turned into rampant cancer. How did the inexplicable happen: her leaving us, loss uniting us? Within us is Valeria, always. What *I* can do now, Antonio adds, his face contorting in pain, I'm able to do because I've been granted a second life. But *she* . . .

As we both know, any description of what's happened will fall wide of the mark. *We are born with the dead: / See, they return, and bring us with them*, wrote T. S. Eliot. That's perhaps as close as I can get.

One recent lunchtime, a young cat very unlike the half-blind one—fluffy tail, pale-green eyes—managed to reach our terrace, having somehow scaled a wall and crept across our upper roof. It tried to enter the house; seeing us step out to investigate, it backed off warily.

I fetched a saucer of ricotta and put it on the terrace. When I returned to the doorway, the cat began eating, and I was able to approach. I made sure to blink, to state in the cat's own language that I intended no harm. After a moment, the cat blinked back. Though I knew it'd soon flee, I found myself hoping I could be a sort-of mother to it, if only for a little while. An oversized, fur- and tail-less simulacrum of the cat's true mother, wherever she might be. Assuming she still lived.

The cat devoured the ricotta, then cleaned itself. Antonio and I watched it take off, a graceful model of self-possession. Would it, like the kitten with the infected eyes, survive whatever awaited it? I hadn't told it outright I hoped so. Not that this mattered; we'd exchanged the speech of acceptance, silent and mutual. And who knew, maybe the cat would come back. Perhaps before long, we'd find it curled quietly in a corner of the terrace. Noting our presence, it would swivel its head, those lovely eyes the color of sea glass . . . I'd blink at it, and it would blink in response.

What its blinking might be saying: Don't make so much of being seen. Try rather to see, however you can.

3. Pleasantly and Well-Suited

THEY'RE DARK BROWN, AS IT TURNS OUT. NOT BLACK LIKE Batman. And small, not much bigger than mice. Exceedingly fast, too—when they fly, I don't hear a whoosh or flap-flap but rather a zippy *SSSssssss* . . . Yet as I learned on our very first night here, bats can also move languorously.

I've been thinking about that night ever since.

Antonio and I were punch-drunk with excitement and fatigue, barely able to eat. I'd fixed us a little salad; we'd washed it down with some Prosecco Antonio found in the fridge (a gift, intentional or not, from our absent landlord), then dragged ourselves up to our bedroom.

A dark-green canvas cloth covers the bedroom windows. Actually, the windows are a pair of glass-paned doors that open onto a balcony. Two hooks, one on each side of the doors, affix the green cloth to the outer wall of the house. Since Antonio is taller than I, it's his job to fasten the cloth in place each night, take it down each morning, and put it up again at noon, to keep the room cool.

On the day of our arrival, the cloth was hooked up. Antonio took it down and tossed it onto the terrace, so we could enjoy the view while we hauled and unpacked our stuff. Hours later, after supper—it was fully dark by then—Antonio went onto the balcony to put up the cloth, and woke a bat tucked into its folds.

Antonio saw nothing. I, however, was in the bedroom, and saw an oval shadow waft slowly across the doorsill into the bedroom.

It passed a few feet from my face. A very large moth, I figured: a sort of compact and noiseless flying lozenge. It seemed to float rather than fly, with no sputter of wings or erratic motion. Hang on, I thought—this thing isn't a moth, or even a bird . . . The word *bat* took several more seconds to arrive.

The creature circled near the ceiling as it tried to get out. At one point it aimed directly at us as we squatted, our arms flailing over our heads. Then it veered and sailed slowly through the bedroom door and down the stairwell. Slamming the door shut, Antonio and I jabbered anxiously in English and Italian, trying to make sense of what'd just occurred. The brisk shaking of the green cloth, we decided, must've launched the bat aloft; it hadn't had the option of slipping away from the cloth on its own schedule. And now it was seeking a hiding-spot.

For a little while, each of us tried unsuccessfully to get the other to go downstairs, find the bat, and shoo it out. Then, too tired to care any longer, we turned off the light and tumbled into bed, not bothering to cover the glass-paned doors with the cloth. *Adrift*, I thought as I lay in the moonlit room: the bat had drifted in without aim or purpose. It wasn't trying to invade our space; it had erred, entering, and simply wanted out. Yet despite the circumstances, the bat's flight had seemed leisurely, as if the creature had all the time in the world.

The next morning we tiptoed downstairs, looked all over, climbed to the third floor, saw nothing, decided against entering the crawl space, and gave up. Somehow, the bat must've fled outside. Or was hiding in the walls of the house.

They're very *retrattili*, Antonio said. They can fold themselves up into nothing, slip under baseboards . . . In any case, it'll find a way out.

Or not, I thought. Or it'll get stuck, and eventually we'll smell it.

But why that strangely easy, unrushed glide?

Since then, whenever I see bats' shadowy forms darting through the air at dusk, keeping mosquitoes at bay, I recall that lone interloper coasting into our bedroom.

Folded in the green cloth, the bat must've imagined itself shrouded from danger. Like an actor behind a theater's thick curtain, her lines memorized and movements mapped, waiting for the preordained rise of dark velvet before stepping onstage and playing her part . . . Then suddenly everything changes, this isn't the right moment, no, something's gone amiss yet the curtain's lifting anyway—*whoosh!*

But that bat was no helpless actor. When it was tossed onstage without warning, its surprise provoked not a mad skitter but a slow-down, a husbanding of its energy. Perhaps the bat expected to meet its end, perhaps to elude it; who can say? The creature's gone now, but its stately passage through our bedroom has left me with a question. Faced with unexpected, unrehearsed perils, will I learn to glide through my own spaces of heart and mind without automatically heightening the drama? Will I be able to waft rather than flail and rush?

Walt Whitman put his finger on the challenge in "To Think of Time," a poem in which he asks: *If I were to suspect death, I should die now, / Do you think I could walk pleasantly and well-suited toward annihilation?* That image of Whitman strolling toward his own extinction like some relaxed flaneur makes me smile. Such was his intent, I suppose—to make me realize how much, despite my boasts to the contrary, I fear time's passage. And how futile my resistance is.

Give me a hand with this thing, calls Antonio.

He's out on the balcony, trying to put up the green cloth. It's definitely a two-person job on this moonless, gusty evening. A summer rainstorm's en route; a few drops spatter us. We wrestle the cloth onto its hooks and step inside the bedroom; when we close the doors, the wind gives a sharp whistle, as though objecting to being shut out.

We should deal with that curtain before dark, Antonio says. Not after.

Yeah, I say. Remember the bat?

You bet!

He smiles, proud of himself. I've recently taught him that expression, which he enjoys; the Italian version, *puoi scometterci* (literally, "you can bet on it"), isn't as zippy.

Porco pipistrello! he adds. Wasn't that evening fun!

He's recently taught me *pipistrello*, the word for bat. When I told him it was dumb that such a wee animal had such a long name, he retorted that at least *pipistrello* wasn't also the name of a stick. What stick, I asked. The one they use in that silly American national sport, he answered.

Living here, I say, I bet we'll be learning all kinds of stuff from animals.

I already have, says Antonio. That cat with the fluffy tail— she got inside the house yesterday, I forgot to tell you . . . I found her in the living room, lying on the blue chair like she owned the place. *Cazzarola!* So you know what? For the next year, I'm gonna pretend *I* own the place, too!

I should try that as well, I think as we climb into bed.

Not just sort-of pretend, though. It'll have to be genuine, this make-believe—a serious game of "as if." I'll need to imagine myself the actual proprietor of this domicile. I'll do it for the sake of expansion: not of property but of self. *As if one fit to own things*, mused Whitman, *could not at pleasure enter upon all, and incorporate them into himself or herself . . .* Incorporate all things, all experiences. *Because all I see and know, I believe to have purport in what will yet be supplied.*

The wind whistles again. We pull the blanket up to our ears. Drops of water ping off the glass doors.

Watch out, *amore*, says Antonio. Here it comes!

Though it's pitch-black in the room, I can tell from his tone that he's smiling. So am I.

Off-leash, the rain scampers across the roof.

4. *Fatti Nostri*

THE MADONNA OF CASTIGLIONE DEL TERZIERE RESIDES IN A miniature one-room edifice made of stuccoed brick, with a terra-cotta roof.

She's about thirty inches tall, wearing a flowing robe with a blue sash. Her head-scarf, like the robe, is white with gold trim. She gazes outward, her expression the classic one of open-eyed humility and contemplation; her two palms lie flat against each other, fingertips upright. Colorful plastic flowers lie at her side, along with what appear to be flora and fauna lodged in glass jars filled with water. The jars' lids have been sealed with gold braid. There's also a red electric light at the front of the alcove, above its door; it reminds me, incongruously, of a whore's beacon.

When was her original home built? No one's sure, although according to a small plaque set into the stucco, it was reconstructed in 1966. Now, more than fifty years later, the Madonna's abode has just been through a remodeling. A new plaque will have to be made, but that can wait. What counts is that this residence is once again sturdy, and the Madonna herself has been touched up, her dignity restored.

Roberto, one of her renovators, says, "I fixed her home so she'll help me stay healthy."

Elide says, "We can all pray better, now that she's got a decent place of her own."

Rina simply smiles, maybe because she's hard-of-hearing and has no idea what's just been said.

The Madonna oversees *la colla*, the piazza that serves as the collective entrance point for Castiglione. Near its connection with the entry road are the houses of Roberto and of Daniel, another of the Madonna's renovators; he and his family are from Romania. At the far end of *la colla* begins the cobblestoned lane that ascends to the upper *borgo*. Lined by four houses on one side and an abandoned farmhouse with a small grazing plot on the other, *la colla* is the unofficial, unglamorous seat of the village. Our collective trash and recycling receptacles are here, as are at least half the village's cats and one of its three dogs. Entering or leaving, residents encounter one another regularly in *la colla*.

Most summer evenings, a small group gathers at the *incipit* of the cobblestone lane. They perch on a low stone wall or on plastic chairs for a few hours of chat, joking about being the village's *dogana*—its Customs, where newcomers must show their documents or tell a good story in order to pass. An aged sign near this gathering point chronicles the village's historical significance during the Renaissance, when castles did the work of defense departments and the *borgo* came into its own as a seat of civil law, one of Florence's key outposts in northern Tuscany.

What the sign doesn't capture is Castiglione's unusual trajectory thereafter.

After several centuries of historical prominence and several more during which the *borgo* gradually ceased to matter to the Florentines or anyone else, its castle—reduced to near-ruin—was purchased in the 1960s and restored by Loris Jacopo Bononi. Obsessed with his native Lunigiana and with literature, Bononi created and curated a remarkable library in the castle. Stacked higgledy-piggledy on the five-hundred-year-old shelves of grand armoires are rare medieval and Renaissance manuscripts, incunabula, and first editions of Dante, Petrarch, and other Italian and Lunigianese authors. The castle contains a culture trove little known outside the region. The aged sign in *la colla* gives no hint that such a pot of book-gold exists, not over some rainbow but right up the hill.

These days, only a dozen or so people (including Antonio and myself) live in Castiglione year-round. Our ranks swell to around thirty when members of families who've long owned houses here return in August for a few weeks of rest and nostalgia. Our oldest long-term permanent residents, Elide and Rina (the latter, at eighty-five, has ten years on the former), hold court in *la colla*: they are its twin queens. Seated on cushions on a stone stoop, they listen as information is traded, questions are raised, judgments passed, arguments settled. A few feral cats venture for handouts. And the Madonna asserts her silent sovereignty.

On a late-August afternoon, while the renovators of the Madonna's abode took a cigarette break, I told Elide about the challenges Antonio's daughter was facing. She'd been trying to wean her twenty-month-old son.

Elide recounted her own daughter's experience with one of her kids, a little girl who would go to kindergarten without a fuss, play and have lunch, return home in the afternoon, and ask to be nursed—not out of hunger but because this was the best way to process social anxiety. Elide mimed the giving of a breast to a baby. *Quasi quattro anni*, she reiterated, brows raised— *almost four years old!* She made one of my favorite Italian gestures: one hand slightly cupped, thumb touching the tips of bunched fingers, the whole performing a forward-backward motion in the air as if to say, *give me a break!*

Clever kid, I said to Elide. *I guess we could all use such help.*

Elide rolled her eyes. I wondered how often she used to pray to the Madonna when children, husband, in-laws, chickens, pigs, and everything else got to be too much for her. On damp, mildew-producing spring days; during winter *temporali* with their stinging rains; while her garden languished under a high summer sun; on gray autumn mornings when nothing stirred but monotony itself: at such times (and they must've been legion), prayer might've been a useful distraction. And might still be helping her now, in moments when she thought, *I may be next to leave.*

The renovation of the Madonna's alcove involved several days' painstaking labor on the part of three men: Roberto, Daniel, and another man, elderly and florid, whose name I never caught. Roberto and Daniel did the lion's share of the work.

To each of them Elide issued supervisory orders. *We need a place for flowers. No, rotate her slightly! A little more to the left. Good! Are you sure about that color?* Rina, the assistant supervisor, simply smiled encouragingly at the workers. The three of them would keep at it, her smile seemed to say. They'd get the job done right, not because Elide was riding herd but because the Madonna was.

The men built a wood-framed glass door for the alcove—a new design element, and a tricky bit of work. The door had to arc at the top, which meant the glass had to be cut and set into its frame with care.

Daniel took it upon himself to do the carpentry work. Roberto ceded this responsibility without argument, admiring as he does Daniel's can-do attitude and energy. Roberto himself is competent in many areas—he cultivates olive trees and makes marmalade from his bountiful plums—but he knew Daniel would fret if anyone else performed the task at hand. Roberto's chatty and can seem oblivious, yet he's canny about people. (When my daughter and wife arrive for a visit, he says, I give them the run of the place. We get along better that way.)

Before the glass-paned door could be installed, the men had to repair and repaint the alcove's stucco interior. Then they fixed the Madonna's chips and cracks, and repainted her from head to toe. To do so, they had to take her out and stand her on the ground, where she could be more easily worked upon and dried in the sun. No one seemed concerned that she was subjected to midday heat. Lunch hour and a short stretch before supper were the only times when all three renovators could convene to accomplish their mission, so everyone agreed that the Madonna would have to deal with the weather.

Once all the repair work was done, the men resituated the Madonna so her position in the alcove would deliver maximum benefits to whoever approached her—even people who wouldn't notice or care about her as they walked by. The men were undertaking this renovation, I slowly realized, not just for themselves but for everyone—known or unknown, locals or strangers, believers or atheists—who visited or lived in the *borgo*. This was not a selfish mission.

Why? I asked Antonio. Why are they putting so much energy into this?

To make their own homes sacred, he answered.

When I asked him what he thought *sacred* meant—not to the Church but to the villagers—he replied that he thought it meant safe.

* * *

The renovation has been finished for a fortnight. Roberto calls to us as we're getting out of our car, groceries in hand. Since his house sits at the far end of *la colla*, opposite Daniel's, they both monitor anyone entering or leaving the village.

Come, Roberto says, you've never seen my garden, have a look. Bring that stuff over here and put it in the shade.

He shows us around. Plum and olive trees descend in neatly terraced rows; a lemon tree boasts large yellow orbs. At the side of the house is an herb garden rife with thyme, rosemary, parsley, and basil. The whole scene gives off an air of calm fecundity.

Roberto offers us a glass of wine. We talk about the renovation project in *la colla*, how efficiently it was done. Roberto praises Daniel—that guy can do just about anything with his hands, he says—and Antonio asks how Daniel's newborn is doing. A light-blue chiffon bow announcing the baby's birth at the start of summer is still wrapped around a stone pillar at the base of Daniel's driveway.

Ah, says Roberto, a frown passing over his face. The kid's doing fine, I suppose. But what a mess . . . Daniel's parents came from Romania right before the birth, and then something happened; they left right after the baby came home from the hospital.

Why, I ask.

Oh, they must've had an argument. I don't know. In any case, they got in their car and drove off the next morning, and that was that. All the way back to Romania!

What did Daniel have to say about it, asks Antonio.

Again Roberto frowns. Not much, he answers. Something about how people just don't understand . . .

He gazes off. *Sono fatti suoi*, he concludes, hands up and palms facing outward. It's Daniel's business.

Antonio and I thank him for the fruit he's given us, collect our groceries, and walk up the lane, both of us quiet. Think of Daniel's wife, I say. Alone in that house all day with a new baby . . .

Yes, says Antonio, it must often be lonely for her. And they must've been counting on help.

The Madonna hasn't been paying sufficient attention, has she, I think. Neither have the rest of us, though. We're all occupied with *fatti nostri*—our own business, our own lives. The sacred gets pressed upon by realities as obdurate and unyielding as the stone wall of Daniel's driveway. That pale-blue bow will soon come down, washed or blown off by rain or wind.

Until the renovation, the Madonna had been looking rather disheveled—no surprise, since she'd been exposed to the elements for an awfully long time. Bits of her gown were chipped; her feet were smudged with dirt. Now she's all spiffed up. But her expression remains the same: neither engaged nor detached.

Who can speak for her, for what she feels? One can only guess. What the villagers would say: *Tu sei benedetta fra le donne, e benedetto è il frutto del ventre tuo*—blessed art thou among women, and blessed is the fruit of thy womb. What I imagine Elide must've said, nursing her third child as the other kids sapped her energy and their father dealt with pigs and cows, fields and tractor: Don't let this one keep wanting the breast! What Daniel's wife must've said when her in-laws left: something in Romanian, expressive of outrage and exhaustion. What Rina might've said, hearing other women's complaints: How is it possible I never married, never had a child?

No one can translate for the Madonna. And perhaps she says nothing original, instead repeating by rote what she's heard since the start of time: *E il settimo giorno Dio terminò la sua opera.* Which is fine—but her renovators want to rest, too, on the seventh day. And they must be thinking, you know, we worked really hard to clean you up. We gave you a nice new door, a fresh paint job, flowers. Now is it safe, your home? And ours? Can you promise us?

I have no dog in this race, as we say in English; I don't pray.

Nonetheless I imagine the Madonna has had to train herself to not be distraught by so much human difficulty around her. To steel herself and dole out help as she can, recognizing that everyone's got their own stuff, *fatti loro*, to attend to— hence the best and only thing she can do is be calm when people come to her with their tales of need or woe, heads bowed before her red-lit door. To listen without judgment, even without reaction.

I was not raised Catholic, and have long ceased feeling the tug of my mildly Protestant upbringing. Yet each day when I pass the Madonna in her refurbished abode, I can't help but note that my neighbors' faith has transmuted doubt, fear, and awe into a tangible counterweight: a local habitation for a sympathetic listener who's always at the ready. I recall, too, how my mother would sometimes ask my siblings and me to go to church with her when we were children. At the time I didn't understand what she could possibly receive from droning Episcopalian sermons and dull hymns that she couldn't get much more happily from the Bach and Mozart she'd ask us to put on the stereo, or the opera she'd tune into on the radio.

My father, a strident nonbeliever, would drive us to church and stay in the car. My siblings and I would guide our mother inside the church and sit with her. Why did she insist upon this—she who didn't do a lot of insisting? I think what she sought was not to affirm belief, but to be lodged momentarily in a physical space expressive of it. To be seated on one of belief's hard benches and sing a few of its songs. To see nothing, yet hear the play of echoes in that high-windowed place, that haven whose ceilings were vaulted.

Rather than words, wrote Philip Larkin, *comes the thought of high windows: / The sun-comprehending glass, / And beyond it, the deep blue air . . .*

The holy girl gleams in the sun. I add a bit of water to the droopy flowers someone left in a vase at the side of the Madonna's home.

Then I remind myself to describe this scene to my mother, next time we speak on the phone. She'll assume the Madonna is housed in the little church up by the castle; she'll picture a regally gilded Mary near an altar. The actual residence— its humble dimensions and location in *la colla*, its droopy flowers—will startle my mother. But isn't that where you park your car, she'll ask. Yes, I'll say, and the Madonna has to suck down exhaust fumes, poor thing! My mother will chuckle incredulously and then begin to cough, short of breath. She's got congestive heart failure. I can pray all I like, but that cough of hers isn't going away.

After tidying up the flowers, I gaze at the Madonna for a moment. As always, she's looking elsewhere, lost in thought, silent as the proverbial tomb. She and I are the only ones present; everyone else has gone inside for lunch.

I close my eyes. What's audible in *la colla*, if I listen for it when no one else is there, is the whispering of the Madonna to herself. It sounds like the murmur of the fruit trees in Roberto's garden. And the incessant wheeze in my mother's chest. Perhaps these sounds are essentially the same: *l'aria della vita*. Along with them I sometimes pick up a contrasting, vivifying echo—that of the brisk intake of air of the three men who, after packing up their tools, stood for a few minutes before the Madonna's home, smoking their rough cigarettes, satisfied with their labor.

5. Takeaway

THE OTHER NIGHT—COOL, DAMP, SOUND-MUFFLING—A FOX ate the two baby geese Raffaella recently purchased.

Raffaella lives in Castiglione's castle. For more than twenty-five years, she's been the consort and helpmate of Loris Jacopo Bononi, the owner. These days, he's rarely out and about. Bononi is ill with cancer; we don't expect him to last long. Dying though he is, he remains the ruling presence in the *borgo*. All of Castiglione's residents view him with a mix of affection, respect, and bewilderment. Slightly built and elegantly dressed, with a hawk's profile and disconcertingly vivid blue eyes, Bononi gives an immediate impression, even in his weakened physical state, of someone living on the edge—of what, one isn't quite sure.

He's shrewd and quick-witted; also short-fused, harshly judgmental, irrational. Given to grand gestures (when younger he threw legendary parties, and he still insists on flying the Florentine flag on his upper terrace), Bononi is capable of touchingly genuine acts of kindness. He likes to make people laugh; he's sweet with children and animals; he cries easily, especially when reciting his own poetry. A showboater? Yes, but an undeniably gifted entertainer as well, whose use of Italian is marvelously idiosyncratic. *La scrittura é il solo segno che superstita un uomo*, Bononi said to us one day—using a nonexistent verb, *superstita*. He'd created it by tinkering with *superstite*, an adjective that means *surviving*. What did he intend by that? *Writing is the only sign that outlasts a person*—and when the sign is defamiliarized, it becomes all the more memorable.

Bononi brought the *borgo*'s castle back to life. By the 1960s the edifice was in near-ruins; at the end of that decade, *il professore* undertook the self-imposed, onerous, and expensive task of restoration.

Several years went into heavy structural work, and years more into gathering every object that would fill the renovated *castello*: books, art, musical instruments, and furnishings, all related in some manner to Lunigiana. This "castle idea," as Bononi calls it—a nexus at once physical and conceptual—is the central reality of his life. It's a gift to himself, of course, but also to his Lunigianese compatriots. His aim has been to restore not only the castle but also a local culture long overlooked.

Without Raffaella's help, however, Bononi couldn't have pulled it off. A spirited woman who's lived with *il professore* since her late twenties, she shares his love of Castiglione. Within a few years of her arrival, Raffaella oversaw the restoration of several houses in the *borgo*, putting her art-historical training to tasteful use. She made it her job to take care of the flowers in the village's main piazza. As she's done for decades, she maintains the castle's interior, hoisting iron bars across its windows' huge wooden shutters each evening and filling its vases with flowers every week. And she assists *il professore* when groups of students or visitors arrive, serving them excellent strong coffee at the end of the tour.

Raffaella knows the history of the castle as no one else does, and her hopes for its future are fully aligned with her partner's.

Still, she's much younger than Bononi—a beautiful woman with a thick mane of dark-chestnut hair, a high bright laugh, and a temper normally checked but occasionally eruptive—and I often wonder how she's navigated her life with him. Though no pushover, she's disinclined to preen; she holds back while he holds forth. Cohabitation must be a tricky balancing act for her, not a fairy tale; *il professore* is, after all, a mythomane.

Raffaella responds strongly to animals, observing their habits as some humans notice others' tics. Like *il professore*, she spends a lot of time alone, and Bononi's death won't be likely to alter that habit. Encounters with people matter to Raffaella, her phone rings a good deal—yet she seems happiest in the company of Mia, her enormous Central Asian sheepdog, who chews on big bones in the castle's upper courtyard and likes to pad up and down the stone stairs to the lower terrace.

Having watched plenty of animals get sick and die, Raffaella is unsentimental about their lives. The violence that often
marks their interactions in the *borgo* is normal for her, can even
make her chuckle. But their fates instruct her nonetheless.

She bought the geese on a whim. They weren't egg-suppliers,
nor were they intended to end up on her table. I think Raffaella
simply felt they'd enliven the scene.

Fluffy white things—more blobs than birds—the geese
used to flee their cage as soon as the door was opened for them
each morning, then waddle and flap into the undergrowth
opposite our house. I'd hear them now and then, scrabbling in
the leaves. Ungainly though they were, they somehow managed not to tumble down the steeply sloped terraces, bounce
off the high wall, and plunge *splat* onto our alley. They were the
borgo's newest survivors, or so we all figured.

At the time of their deaths, Raffaella had owned the goslings about three weeks. She'd kept them in the garden because
it seemed the logical spot—verdant, quiet, safe. Mia wasn't
a danger to them; she sniffed them a bit, then ignored them.
Mia often romps during daylight along the garden's perimeter,
her footfall like a giant's. Sometimes she disappears into the
deepest brush, and we'll hear Raffaella calling for her, often to
no avail. Mia knows how to hunker down, stay still, mute her
panting, and outwait her owner.

The goslings were less adept at hiding. Though small, they
couldn't help but thrash and peep. With their high-pitched,
oddly cadenced cries, the pair seemed always to be lobbing

questions at the world: Where *are* we, how to get *out* of here, *what* is that dog *up* to, *who* will *care* for *us*? They lacked any talent for silence.

For my own part, I have been practicing wordlessness.

It is not a usual human art. Most people lack regular opportunities to try it. Yet wordlessness can be undertaken, I've discovered, as an exercise, with times and places designated for its performance if improvisation isn't practicable. It's quite doable in a mostly uninhabited medieval village that presents irregular, easily avoided opportunities for social interaction.

Truth is, I've lately had little need for speech. Not even with Antonio, who, like me, spends much of each day at his desk. I'm at work on my third novel, and Antonio on fiction of his own. In addition, we're under contract for a translation: the final short-story collection of Antonio Tabucchi, a recently deceased Italian writer we both love. The two of us toggle between our individual productions and the deadline for a book we're making together.

We brew tea several times daily, and speak if we have to. When translating, of course, we've no choice but to talk, argue, laugh, and look up words in several dictionaries. Otherwise, we mostly stay silent. This quiet of ours isn't itself disquieting; in our shared life it's an option, not a habit. We choose it so we can work in peace—Antonio on the second floor and myself in the third-floor garret, where raindrops drum softly on the roof. Our silence gets broken when we meet in the kitchen: meals are for eating and talking.

Being wordless is not, of course, the same as being heed-less or incurious. Animals show us this: they may not all be as inquisitive as cats, but they can't survive without the instinct to question, silently or aloud. Before their demise, Raffael-la's goslings spent the better part of each day in an interroga-tory mode. Unable to interpret what they might be asking while they waddled around the garden, I was struck nonetheless by how persistently the goslings launched their squeaky queries. To my ear, those solicitations sounded equal parts fearful and raucous. And in retrospect (once they'd ended for good) bravely relentless as well.

As for my own questions these days: *Who is it can tell me who I am* seems less central than *Can someone tell me what to do?* I don't mind that no single, clear answer is forthcoming. The usual responses provided by my routines at my univer-sity—classes, meetings—carry no weight now, nor do direc-tives come in the form of social obligations here in Castiglione. There's no *caffé* in the village to pull me from my lair. I don't feel guilty if I stay home all day.

Routines stripped of a social aspect become interior, the self's negotiations with time's passage.

Shall I (my self asks itself, at least once a day) spend time staring at that tree over there, around which a hawk with an impressive wingspan is circling as if to land? Or (anxious now about wasting time) shall I at least wash the dishes and do the laundry while I'm puzzling over some problem with my writing? Or (expanding and complicating my choices) shall I attempt to verbalize the sensation accompanying a recent realization that my mother isn't guaranteed to celebrate her ninetieth birthday? Not that *she* feels the need to live another couple of years. The realization is as much about myself as about my mother—which is to say, wouldn't it be nice for *me* if she'd hang on till I get home? Can't she wait two more years so we can cross the border together, she into her nineties and I, her firstborn, into my sixties?

A related query arises. For my mother, isn't the stale routine of birthdays—those annual markers of time, like colored stripes in the sand of the hourglass—less pleasing than the ritual of pushing the "run" button on her audiobook player, in hopes of hearing a narrative that can sustain attention?

Which reminds me: I must go online and browse the Library for the Blind's "Talking Book" audio catalogue. Time to send my mother some more titles.

She's just finished *Anna Karenina*. She never read it when she was young.

Well, she told me on the phone the other day, now *there's* a book.

Our friend Benni has ALS, and has been wordless and motionless for years.

He lives in Cremona, where he and Antonio were school friends; they've known one another since boyhood. His home, which has been in his family for generations, is an old villa next to a medieval church; it sits behind walls, beautifully private, invisible to passersby. Benni's like that, too. The nephew of a well-known lawyer—and himself a prominent *avvocato*, trusted and admired—Benni lacked for nothing until he became ill. He knew plenty of people but grew close to very few. Now his mind is intact, but he can move none of his muscles, only his eyes, and those only a little. The maintenance work for his body is done by both machines and humans. He has a breathing machine, a feeding tube, a catheter, and physical therapy to prevent muscular atrophy and alleviate bedsores.

Until recently, Benni communicated with a laser-equipped computer trained to read his gaze and translate his eyes' movements into letters and words. For a time, his special computer ensured he wasn't completely cut off from the people he's close to. Benni's family lives with him, so in one sense he's not alone. But of course he is: such an illness makes solipsism unavoidable.

During our several visits with him in 2011, Benni was still able to "talk" with us.

We'd enter his room and find him where he always is, in bed, motionless as a corpse but making his usual mechanical-breathing sounds. We'd kiss his cheek and touch his arms, smiling at him; then we'd recount our news, or update him on the doings of mutual friends. Benni's eyes would gleam and blink (a year ago, blinking was easier for him), and despite the immobility of his face, his gaze would let us know he was glad we were there.

Listening to our tales, Benni would write with his eyes. This would take time. A few minutes after, say, a joke about an old schoolmate or a comment about politics, Benni's computer would interrupt the conversation (if it might be called that) to offer, in a tinny, artificially high male voice, Benni's response to the joke or comment we'd already left behind. Those computer-voiced words of his were invariably trenchant, ironic, humorous. Benni's mind and eyes were incessantly tracking and responding: he was working double-time, in the present and in delayed mode. Each time Antonio and I said goodbye to him, I'd feel my heart clench in awe of his capacity to communicate.

The disease wasting his body has recently brought Benni's computer usage to a halt. His sentences used to be cleanly typed; then they started to sputter across the screen, littered with typos, sometimes incomplete or incoherent. Now they've ceased. Fortunately, his wife knows exactly how his various caregiving machines function, and she can read Benni's gaze in her own way—unlike the computer, which required Benni to blink intentionally. She is dedicated to him, rarely leaving the house for more than a few hours. I wonder what's harder for her now: the mechanics of taking care of so profoundly hampered a body, or the frustration and sorrow of being cut off from dialogue with a mind so unfettered and expressive before illness jailed it.

She and Benni have two adult sons in their twenties, both living at home, playing a waiting game with death. Whenever I imagine I understand the sons' muted anguish, I stop and chastise myself for the comparison. It's one thing to watch a parent go slowly blind, and another to sense that the parent is drifting out to sea while you're ashore—and you can shout till you're hoarse, but you won't be able to reel him in.

A few days after the fact, Raffaella told us what happened to the goslings.

They'd hidden somewhere, per usual. Locating them was always a production. We'd hear Raffaella making *pea-pea-pea* noises in the undergrowth, trying to get the geese to answer loudly enough for her to hear and find them. Then we'd hear her shooing them toward their cage. She knew she should've locked them up for the night, but that evening, she simply hadn't felt like tracking them down to cage them. The next morning, she'd found nothing more than a few feathers, bloodied.

As she recounted the story, I could hear the sorrow and regret in her tone. Yet it seemed to me that since the goslings had always sought to escape, sooner or later they'd have released themselves and dashed off, aiming for freedom—which in their case (given the roaming fox) was synonymous with being killed. Maybe Raffaella should have resigned herself to being their eventual if unwitting executioner.

There's no takeaway from all this, nothing to learn. No central truth about what to *do* with the fact of death that isn't already at some level known, though the knowledge feels useless. Your day comes, it's your turn, accept it: what are such bromides to the goslings, or to Benni?

Sometimes when Antonio and I pass each other in the kitchen or living room of our damp stone abode, we'll suddenly embrace each other fiercely, like two people on a boat who have a simultaneous intuition of imminent foundering. A strange sensation, this, since the boat of our marriage makes us both happy. It's not the love, though, or the marriage, but the vessels—our bodies—that will founder. And though we might squeak in odd cadences, or call out *pea-pea-pea*, or yell or yak, such speech will change nothing.

Antonio calls Benni's wife this evening, to find out how he's doing. Same as when we saw him last, she reports.

Benni's immured in his head, and has no say about that or anything else. Wordlessness isn't a choice for him. He can't participate in the upkeep of his body, and the people around him must guess at how he's maintaining his mind. Until he was deprived of the use of his eyes to activate his computer, Benni spent as much time as possible writing. He composed personal essays, reminiscences, and brief sketches of his life. He didn't write about other people, except incidentally, nor did he deliver answers to questions such as *who am I* or *what should I do?* Instead, he wrote out, blink by blink, various vivid physical experiences, returning in his mind to the time when he was able to have them. He wrote about his military service, rendering it in scenes both absurd and comic; about arduous travels in Afghanistan and India when he was in his thirties; about going to China in fruitless search of a cure for his disease. He wrote about childhood games. About food. About the body in motion.

Benni isn't afraid of his cage, his writing tells us. Nor is he trying to release himself from it or anything else. If he feels terror, he has said nothing of it. His gaze seems at times smiling, at other times appraising, at other times recalling, reliving, renewing his stash of memories. His sight appears to be mostly inward-directed. About love he has written very little; the word needs or bears, it seems, no saying.

Benni won't die in the cold. He'll die in his bed, unto himself, having seen and communicated what he could.

6. Inside, Outside

THIS MORNING, I FOUND BIG BOY, THE BLACK-AND-WHITE dandy who visits us from time to time, curled on the bed in the guest room. He'd snuck in from the terrace and slunk upstairs.

Skittish and lean, Big Boy lives in a state of constant vigilance. Lately he's been favoring one leg, the right rear one. It was a relief to find him curled into a ball on the bed, his hurt leg splayed outward, the rest of him indifferent to inspection. I stood and gazed at him, keeping still so he'd feel safe.

Big Boy hasn't ever been accepted by the other cats in the village. Perhaps that's because he's not sufficiently aggressive. He began showing up at our house not long after our arrival, a sleek creature who'd eat rapidly while hissing either at Tristana—the fluffy-tailed cat who more or less adopted us after that first visit of hers—or at whichever human hand was proffering food. These days, Big Boy allows himself to be petted, though he's always wary.

When we leave, who will feed him? There's Rina, who's got a dozen cats showing up each morning for her meager gruel of bread and broth. Nearly deaf, Rina won't hear Big Boy's cries of hunger, or notice he's having a hard time getting to the food bowl because he's limping, or because the other cats chase him away. There's Raffaella, but she has her hands full with her own passel of felines; they're very territorial, and will make it impossible for Big Boy to dine at the castle. Nobody else in the village feeds the feral cats. Lamed and ostracized, Big Boy will die when the cold weather arrives. Or so I fear.

Big Boy is frightened of humans, yet he knows if he appears on our terrace, Antonio and I will supply food and relief from the other cats. Sometimes, he's able to suppress his fear and enter our home.

Almost all the felines down in *la colla* are different: they don't mind people, but they always remain outdoors. Going against their own grain disturbs them more than having to hunt for food or deal with aggressors. They won't violate their feral nature by entering kitchens or climbing onto beds. They'd rather go hungry.

Which is best, I wonder: finding a way to hedge one's bets, as Big Boy occasionally does, or insisting on personal authenticity at all costs? Making oneself enter a frightening space and then figuring out how to stay there, or tolerating intense, chronic difficulty so as to remain detached? Is there a middle ground?

* * *

A few years before her fortieth birthday, my mother was told about the unusual eye disease that would leave her completely blind. Maybe in a few months, maybe a few years—the specialists couldn't say how long it would take.

This diagnosis came out of the blue. By then she had three young children; at nine or thereabouts, I was the oldest. Mom needed a game plan. I'm sure she knew my father would help her, always; but her game plan would have to start with an inner set of rules, concrete routines of self-discipline. I imagine her sitting herself down, head between hands, contemplating how to get through without falling apart. To keep sanity and family intact. Step one would be key, a nonnegotiable order she'd give herself daily: *no complaining about it.* In effect, that meant *no talking about it.*

Whatever their personalities, most cats vocalize in some manner when scared or distressed. My mother was and is a rare cat: she's consistently opted for silence. My siblings and I have never conversed with her at any length about what happened to her and the rest of us as her eyesight dimmed, then ended. Right from the start, we sensed that if we tried digging deeper, we'd be jeopardizing Mom's emotional balance.

It took the better part of ten years for her sight to fail completely. During that time, she combined two basic strategies for survival—that of Big Boy, and that of the cats in *la colla.* Entering the fearful space of blindness because she had no choice, she found her own ways, practical and personal, of coping with it. She learned Braille; she learned to use a cane; she learned to be guided by Seeing Eye dogs. She learned to memorize room arrangements, to fold paper bills in her wallet according to denomination, to bake bread. She already knew how to cook, knit, type, and play the piano; she learned to do these things afresh, without sight—and, over time, to handle a food processor, a loom, a voice-activated computer, and potters' clay. But she rarely let herself talk about the emotional consequences of her experience, and never in detail. She stayed outside, beyond the lures and limits of speech.

"My Cat Major," a brief, deceptively light poem by Stevie Smith, describes how the eponymous feline—a bird-hunter who *ranges where no one can see*—is forever escaping detection. Major is able to ascend the iron rungs of an attic ladder with one swift kick. *How can this be done?* the poet marvels. *It is a knack*, an inexplicable feat. Equally inexplicable are Major's undertakings. *And what is he at, my fine cat?* As he ranges around the attic, what's his business, what's that cat up to?

No one can see, the poem ends. Which is how Major wants it.

More challenging for me than my mother's reticence has been my own.

I taught myself to obey our household's implicit rule of silence. Moving through junior high and into high school, I seldom spoke with either of my parents about what Mom's inevitable loss of sight was like, either for them or for myself. In those moments during my teenage years when Mom and I knocked heads over other matters—occasionally irritating, injuring, or disappointing each other, as mothers and daughters do—I regretted any lapse on my part into angry or agitated speech. What right did I have to it, after all?

This pattern of remorse and self-censorship continued into adulthood. So what if, during my twenties, my mother was judgmental about my first serious boyfriend, or my search for freelance work instead of a "real" job, or my lack of desire to have kids? So what if, as I journeyed through my thirties, she sometimes expressed opinions that seemed snobbish, ignorant, or out of touch with my own realities? Suck it up, I told myself. What sort of daughter accuses her blind mother of not seeing her?

Once I hit my late thirties, I understood it was I who'd been having vision problems, though not of the physical variety. The fog cleared when I gave myself permission to do what I wanted to do—finish the novel I'd begun several years earlier—and thus break the lock of silence: not Mom's but my own. I stopped longing to tell my mother how I'd felt during her slide into blindness; it wasn't her business and shouldn't be her concern. And I quit wishing for her to talk about it, though my curiosity (too mild a word for an interest in something so intimate) never ebbed. If silence served her best, so be it. She'd come through her loss; like Major the cat, she had a knack. As for where she'd ranged—well, that was for her to know and me to guess. And her ranging wasn't over.

On the afternoon I laid my just-published book, its pages smelling lightly of ink, in my mother's lap, I knew she realized

I'd just handed her my firstborn. I wouldn't be having children; I'd be having books—writing them, that is, in addition to reading and teaching them.

I'd recently entered my forties and ended my first marriage; before long, I'd be starting my first teaching job. Unsurprisingly, the news that my marriage was over had distressed my parents. When I told them, my mother asked if I was sure I didn't want children. It's not too late—can't you imagine it at all? she'd said, clearly bewildered and worried. No, I told her, I couldn't. Not that I hadn't tried: urged by my ex-husband's genuine desire for a family, for a time I'd wanted to want a kid. But that wasn't the same, I'd realized, as seeking parenthood for myself. Such a desire can't be concocted.

At that, my mother had backed off. It's your life, she'd concluded with no hint of opprobrium. Like her own inner realm, Mom's tone suggested, mine was not to be trespassed—by her or anyone else. It was private terrain, risky for others to enter. She'd stay out.

Holding my brand-new book in her lap for a few moments, my mother turned it this way and that, checking its textures and dimensions. Then she laid it carefully next to her, atop a boldly checked wool pillow with big tassels at each corner.

She'd woven the cover for that pillow on a large wooden loom she'd owned for a decade or so, until her stiff joints made the craft too uncomfortable to continue practicing. Throws and pillow covers, placemats, a shawl for me, a skirt for my sister, a bedspread for my brother—Mom made a great deal of beautiful fabric in her middle years. Although her weaving teacher helped her with patterns and colors, the labor was all hers.

Shutting my eyes, I pictured her loom's alternately raised warp threads. In my mind I could still hear the soft, regular thud of the harness, smell the wool, see the shuttle passing back and forth. The task of keeping all the threads evenly taut was tricky for my mother, but she'd gradually mastered it. She'd spent long days readying her loom to produce each new design and pattern—checks and stripes, plaids and tweeds— which she'd dream up herself, then refine with her teacher's assistance. Now and then she'd ask my siblings and me to assess certain color combinations: were they as she'd imagined? Was the blue like that of sky or sea? The green dark as pine, or lighter like grass? The yellow brighter or paler than the color of butter?

Reopening my eyes, I saw my mother stroking my book once more, the fingers of one hand fanning gently over its cover.

I can't wait to read this, she said.

She meant *have it read aloud to me*, of course. I'd need to find someone to record the novel for her—a professional reader with a nice clear voice. But Mom meant something else, too, and on that afternoon she intended for me to hear it clearly: *I'm your mother, I read what you write, my blindness has nothing to do with this.*

She didn't ask what the book was about, for I'd already told her. It wasn't about our family, at any rate. Although, come to think of it, that wasn't really true—the novel's implicit subject was silence . . . Acknowledging the obviousness of something I'd overlooked, I felt a light sweat break out on my forehead. What exactly would my mother make of my book?

I wish, I told her, that I had time to read it to you myself.

I wish you did, too, she replied. But you don't, and anyhow, you should be working on your next one. Are you?

Yeah, Mom, I am, I answered.

She was aiming, I knew, to buck me up. Why then did I have to feel goaded by her? And as for the distrust I thought I detected in her voice, was it really there, or was I simply hearing my own self-doubt?

You don't want to talk about the next book, she added. Which is fine. As long as you're actually writing it.

Boy, Ma, I said, trying for a jokey tone. You sure don't wanna cut me any slack, do you? My first one's just off the press—can't I take a little time to regroup?

We-ell, she drawled. No rest for the wicked, I suppose.

Her shoulders rose and fell in an exaggerated shrug; she was getting into the spirit of the game. Testing me.

Uh, Ma, I thought it was *weary*—no rest for the *weary*, I said.

Oh for heaven's sake, my mother retorted, chuckling. Who *isn't* tired?

Hearing her say that, I flashed onto a line in Galway Kinnell's poem "Wait," one of my favorites: *But no one is tired enough.*

The poem is about loss. About how in its aftermath, we must learn patience and trust time. *Only wait a while and listen.*

There's a music, says the poem, in certain kinds of pain, a music *of looms weaving all our loves again*—restitching the torn fabric, pulling threads taut once again—and we need to hear it. *Rehearsed by the sorrows*, that music will eventually spend itself. But this doesn't matter; we still have to wait, and listen.

You'll do it, my mother stated quietly, as if sensing the moment wasn't really right for the game. It could wait.

Moments, I thought. This moment and others: the tension of warp and weft, love woven and rewoven. Taking my mother's hand, I bounced it lightly up and down in the palm of my own: an old, shared, wordless gesture of connection.

I will, I said.

Like all the cats in the *borgo*, Big Boy avoids dogs. Huge Mia in particular terrifies him.

A few months back, Mia was in the habit of taking Raffaella's cats' newborns—at one point there were nearly a dozen kits from different litters—and trotting around with them in her mouth. Mia wasn't trying to maul or hurt them; she just seemed to like carting them here and there. Using her front teeth, she'd seize the kits by the napes of their necks, sometimes giving one a little shake, as if it were a prized toy, before depositing it somewhere. We all feared necks would be broken, but that never happened. As they grew, the kits learned to flee where Mia couldn't reach them.

One of the female cats in the castle, quite thin before pregnancy, delivered three or four beautifully blue-eyed kits who never stopped crying from the moment they were born. They didn't grow much; they staggered around, crying and crying. One morning, white-faced, Raffaella reported to me that she'd found the kits' decapitated bodies on her back terrace, their heads . . . she'd stopped describing, instead making a gesture with her hands: *What could I do?*

I wondered aloud if it might've been Mia who'd committed the crime, playing too hard with the kittens, but Raffaella said no, it was the mother: she'd torn their heads off, she couldn't take the wails anymore, she knew her offspring weren't going to make it. She was the only one who could've done it. No fox had ever ventured up to the castle terrace, and Mia was inside the whole night.

We'll never know what got twisted inside that mother cat's head, I said to Antonio after recounting what'd happened.

Don't think about it, he said. It's over now.

At least I have one, I said. A mother, I mean. You know, Raffaella was only sixteen when she lost hers . . . She said all the other cats at the castle, especially the females, are spooked by what happened. I bet she's feeling pretty rattled herself.

Loris will write a poem about it, Antonio said. That's how *he* deals with stuff.

True, I said. Which may help him. But I don't know about Raffaella . . .

Encountering her in *la colla* later in the day, I realized Raffaella didn't actually need consoling. She'd recognized there was nothing anyone could've done; she was letting it go. And Mia, she said, needed a good romp. Cooped inside during the rain-filled midday, the dog was restless now that the sun had come out again—so the two of them were going up to the high meadows of Logarghena. Mia had already clambered into the backseat of the car.

Up there, said Raffaella, the air's so bright and fresh. I need it, to clear my head. And Mia will tear around and chase sticks, just like a puppy! On an afternoon like this, you can see all the way to Corsica from there . . .

That enormous emptiness, as Kinnell writes in "Wait," *asks to be filled*.

7. Go Tell Your Father

TWO MURDERS AND A SUICIDE.

Quite a surprise, this news. We'd no idea that our *borgo* had been the site of such drama. Not recent drama, but still . . .

Elide tells us the stories as she sits in *la colla*, waiting for her friend Rina—with whom she oversaw the renovation of the Madonna—to make her way slowly down from her apartment. Rina lives by herself on the second floor of a house partway up the main lane; weather permitting, Elide joins her each afternoon for a few hours of outdoor chat and surveillance. The elderly widow of a *contadino* who, before his death several decades ago, managed the small farm below the village walls where Elide still resides, this woman with thick white hair and brilliant azure eyes is the *borgo*'s newscaster.

One murder, she explains, was committed by a man who, off his rocker to begin with, grew enraged when his wife asked him to hand her a tool for some task she was performing. He picked up a block of wood and cracked her head open with it. I try not to picture the whole scene, but can't help imagining at least the start of it: the wife saying something like *dammi quello martello*—give me that hammer—and extending one hand carelessly toward her husband, while the other hand holds a nail in place on the wall. The wife thinks she's in the middle of hanging a watercolor; they are standing next to the fireplace, the woodpile . . .

The other murder occurred when a man who'd been dumped by his betrothed killed her as she stood staring out a window of the house they'd shared. The view from the window must've been lovely; the woman would've seen the rolling foot-hills of the Appennini, the valley, maybe even the Alpi Apuani in the distance. The man was standing outside. He saw her gazing— not at him but at the church—and took aim and shot her. Again I imagine the scene prompting the act: the woman must've told the man what he didn't want to hear; he'd stormed out; she was left alone to gaze out the window at the church, from which (she was musing) God or Jesus or Mary or some saint or other *ought* to step forth to help her, though none felt close at hand. Only pain did—and fear of her ex-fiancé with his temper . . .

Elide's a fatalist, Antonio says to me after we've bid her good afternoon. She accepts these tales of violence; they don't really shock her. *People can get crazy around here*—that was Elide's prefatory comment, before her narration began. Her half-smile registered not amusement but acceptance: no point being baf-fled, this is just how things sometimes go.

* * *

Then there was the suicide, which took place roughly thirty years ago. I ponder the event as we walk up the lane to our house.

Elide's father-in-law shot himself in her house.

Her husband was out in the fields, per usual. The mother-in-law was in the house but not present in the bedroom where the act took place. It was Elide's ten-year-old daughter who entered the room and found her *nonno*, who'd propped a rifle between foot and jaw and pulled the trigger.

Such a mess, Elide says, shaking her head, you wouldn't believe it. I had to send my son to tell my husband what happened—I couldn't go, I had the girl to deal with, and my mother-in-law . . . And then we had to spend close to a million lire in court! That's close to two thousand euro, a lot of money. To prove he hadn't been *murdered* by one of us!

Do you know why he did it, we ask.

Elide shrugs. He had asthma and emphysema, she answers.

That's it? I ask, incredulous. He wasn't dying of something?

No, she says, and shrugs again. A million lire, she repeats. The whole thing such a mess. And for my girl . . . it wasn't good.

It most assuredly wasn't, I silently agree.

Then there's her brother. I try to picture it: the boy trotting out to the pig shed, calling *Papa! Papa!* The father not noticing or hearing at first, then stopping whatever he's doing—feeding the animals, washing out the slop—to stare at his boy, who's very agitated and yelling something absurd: *Nonno's dead, Nonno shot his head off!* That boy, grown now like his sister, must still be seeing the confused anger on his father's face, still be hearing his outburst—*porca Madonna, what are you saying?* Still unsure, all these years later, which was worse: the event itself, or having to deliver the news to a man who, in the instant of hearing it, was transformed from father to son himself, a stunned boy.

Of course such things happen all over the world, not just in remote Italian villages. I'm scornful of the crazy-villagers trope, the mythologizing of violence in small rural communities, as if such places are inherently predisposed to it. Hardly. It happens anywhere, everywhere.

Outside Denver, Colorado, for instance. In *La Repubblica* we read that a man walked into a packed movie theater—the new Batman film was being screened—and started firing. Killed a dozen people and wounded close to forty others, including an infant. Fancied himself the Joker; dyed his hair red for the role. Amassed such an arsenal of guns and ammunition in his apartment that the authorities say they'll have to blow up the whole booby-trapped place, rather than risk sending personnel to clear it out.

Do we know why he did it? Was he dying of something? Perhaps. Of something in his mind, though we'll never be sure what it was. In any case, he's one of those people who submit without warning to their demons, and do their bidding. Here in Castiglione, no one's heard of the Joker, and ordering boxes of bullets by mail is well-nigh impossible. One can, however, easily get one's hands on a block of wood, and a hunting rifle's not too hard to find. It's just a matter of what the demons say to do, and when they give their orders.

Elide's stories get me thinking, not just about acts of violence I'd like to label parlous or ludicrous and be done with (though of course nothing's that simple), but about the need for drama in the first place.

Come up for coffee! Rina calls as we pass beneath her house the next day. Rina's front windows give onto the village's main lane. It's hard to avoid her if she's on the lookout for company; she's old and lonely, and *we* are drama, for her. Come up and talk to me, she means. Come tell me something I can't see on TV, haven't heard fifty times already from Elide, would like to hear from my niece or nephew if they'd bother to visit, which they don't very often, since I'm their spinster aunt and they have no time for me—as I understand, for I'd feel the same were I in their shoes . . . Come enliven the looping-back-on-themselves days I have left! Come tell me something I can feel strongly about!

It's different when I call my mother.

She admits she has little in the way of news for me, and is eager to hear mine. (*The other cat*, she asks, *not the one you call Tristana—the dandy, Big Boy, is that his name? Does he still hiss at Tristana when you feed the two of them?*) Yet although she takes my stories seriously and listens with attention, my mother knows how to detach as well as to engage.

Her heart attack and broken pelvis have recalibrated her expectations. She's focused on her day-to-day experience, which, boring though it mostly is, nonetheless validates the fact that she's no longer lost in the haze of medications that clouded her thinking and feeling for months. Her wit's fully in place: she enjoys jokes and tales of folly. I make sure to save up "you won't believe what X did" vignettes, to make her snigger. (She howls when I tell her about a funny bumper sticker: *Jesus would slap the shit out of you*.)

But she can take only so much information about the outside world before growing tired. And her hearing's worsening. She's worn aids for a while, but they're not helpful when she's in a conversation with more than two or three people; the voices' volumes and timbres compete, confusing her. When she finds herself in a group—family, friends, it doesn't matter—Mom is adept at dropping out without making anyone feel awkward. Sitting silently, hands in lap, she offers a bemused half-smile while other people produce words. Unless the topic really absorbs her, she's content to let it go.

My siblings and I check in on Mom in person or by phone, as we've always done. It's the steadiness that matters. As a family of adults, we've never communicated frequently; weekly check-ins are the norm. My parents neither expect nor want more. But when my siblings or I get busy and a fortnight passes between calls, my mother's aware of it.

My father notices such gaps, but not as keenly. Not that they're discussed: Mom's the last person in the world to remind her kids to call. When I forget, as I sometimes do, the remorse I feel is like no other; it doesn't go away even after I phone and talk with her. It accretes. Sometimes I feel I'm storing it up, perversely, in anticipation of her death, so that it will break over my head in a huge wave and wash me away.

Grief will do that instead, I expect. But I don't yet know what that icy water will feel like. Remorse is familiar.

My mother has never needed theatricality from her family—no passion plays or tragedies.

Her life has been filled with its own quiet forms of drama, starting with retinitis pigmentosa and continuing with the gradual loss of most of her hearing. Debilitating arthritis plus several falls have led inevitably to her current wheelchair-bound state. All more than enough to make even a reasonable person think, now and then, about staving in somebody's face with a log, or blasting somebody out the window, or filling one's coat pockets with stones and marching straight to the nearest river.

I've never asked my mother if she's had such fantasies. Now and then she's cracked a little, and something shows through a chink in her armor. Mostly, though, she's unbreachable. I can count on the fingers of one hand the number of times I've heard my mother articulate anything having to do with her body and its woes.

She can be surprisingly hard-hearted. It's not her default setting, but it's not an aberration, either. Mom can handle only so much evidence of troubled passages or rocky moments before changing the subject. Dilemmas of work or romance, bouts of anxiety: such challenges have generally elicited from her little more than a shrug and a smile. Lapses in confidence— her kids', her husband's—are for her close to unseemly; she has no patience for failures of resolve. *After great pain, a formal feeling comes*, wrote Emily Dickinson. *A Quartz contentment, like a stone –*

My grandmother Nell was a different bird.

Nell was three weeks shy of her hundredth birthday when she died, of natural causes, in a hospital near her home in New Jersey. She lived in a marvelous house on a steep hill over-looking the Delaware River—the kind of place children love to visit, with narrow staircases, a second-story porch, and an attic straight out of a storybook, dim and book-stuffed, where my grandmother slept. The view from her porch was a bit like ours in Castiglione: trees everywhere, a lush, susurrating swath of green. There were orange daylilies clustered at the top of Nell's driveway, just like those a half-mile down the road from us here. The riverbank on the other side of the Delaware, *across the way*, was in Pennsylvania—a fact that fascinated me when I was young. I loved the notion of two states divided by flowing water, a river in neither one place nor the other.

A year or so before her death, Nell tried to kill herself. To do so, she implicated several family members in the act. First she called my mother—her daughter-in-law— and announced her intention. My mother called my father, who was at work— in a classroom nearly two hours away, teaching math at a pri-vate day school on the Upper East Side of Manhattan. (I picture a schoolboy knocking on his classroom door, politely advising him to go to the headmaster's office. There, a nice pearl-earringed secretary would explain that his wife had just called, sounding a little agitated . . .) In the meantime my mother phoned her only sibling, Katie, who lived a half hour from my grandmother. Katie drove over. The front door was unlocked, so she entered the house and went upstairs and found my grandmother, alive though not fully lucid, in a bathtub full of reddened water.

The hospital social worker assigned to her case described Nell's attempt as "non-trivial." It was intentional, not an accident, yet seemed not to have been undertaken so she'd definitely succeed.

It soon emerged, once Nell began talking (and she was a great talker, always), that she'd been less hell-bent on offing herself than on getting everyone's attention, my father's in particular. She wasn't happy about how she was being managed by him in her old age. Theirs was a contorted relationship, and this was the final kink in a chain of conflict and mutual misunderstanding.

Her act messed with my father's mind, needless to say. It messed with mine as well, since I was quite close to Nell. Yet I hadn't had to play Katie's role and call the ambulance, haul Nell out of the tub, and wrap towels around her wrists. Nor had I had to play my mother's role, that of the person most punished in this drama: the one who could do nothing but inform others. The one whose nose was rubbed in her powerlessness.

Afterward, Nell tried to explain to all of us what she'd been thinking and feeling, but we couldn't get it. Our shock, anger, and sorrow foreclosed any real possibility of understanding. You should've seen it, she said accusingly, I've been trying to tell you . . . (Those lovely dreadful lines from another Stevie Smith poem come to mind: *I was much too far out all my life / and not waving but drowning.*)

After a bit, we all stopped speaking of the matter. Whatever chance there might've been for mending the rift vanished when, eleven months or so after her suicide attempt, she began to have trouble breathing, was taken to the hospital, and died peacefully a few days later, in her sleep, as any ordinary ninety-nine-year-old lady might do. She was cremated and her ashes scattered in her garden, as she'd requested.

To nobody's surprise, my mother wanted no part of that valedictory ritual. It was undertaken by my father, who executed Nell's wish in considerable haste.

I can still picture him in his mother's rectangular flower bed, armed with a bucket and, briefly, an old rake from the garden shed. The rake's crooked tines were barely able to scratch the soil; after a bit, my father replaced the useless implement with a rusty but sturdy spade. He worked alone. I stood at the front door and watched him fling the bucket's contents here and there—unable to decide if this laying-to-rest of a parent's clumpy dust was more comic than pitiful, or vice versa. In any case, he soon got the job done, and washed his hands of her.

* * *

Teach us to care and not to care: that wonderful line from T. S. Eliot's "Ash Wednesday" comes to mind as I visualize my grandmother.

Though the poem ends with a prayer to the spirits of fountain, garden, river, and sea, it's really a poem about private demons and their lures. Eliot's answers to them—his Christian sureties, doubt-tinged though they may be—have never satisfied me. Demons don't bother with the mind and its gymnastics; they go for the emotional jugular. They turn strong feeling upon itself, weaponizing it for their own purposes.

I've always loved that poem. And I have Nell to thank for it. One mild summer afternoon when I was a teenager, my grandmother sat me down at her small kitchen table, opened her dog-eared copy of Eliot's *Collected Poems*, and tracked "Ash Wednesday" with her forefinger. *Teach us to sit still / Even among these rocks*, she murmured. The words riveted me; I repeated them silently to myself, aware as I did so that I, like Nell, rarely ceased moving. In that moment all I wanted (and I wanted it with every molecule in me) was to stop: to be able to sit still.

Yet the prospect was terrifying, for it meant I'd have to confront *these rocks*. Although I could only guess what they might signify for Nell, I already knew what they were for me. *These rocks*: words and acts that couldn't be undone, entrances and exits blocked by error and folly. Rehearsal, it seemed, wasn't rehearsal at all, but actual performance; and in an eye's blink the curtain would fall, our lives would be over and done with—

Listen to the whole thing now, said Nell.

She started at the beginning and read it through, beautifully. When she arrived once more at *these rocks*, a raw anxiety coursed through me. What if I bungled my life's chances, or, worse, became too scared or sad to try?

Suffer me not to be separated, my grandmother intoned, concluding the poem's final prayer, *and let my cry come unto Thee.* Then she stood and began busying herself with kettle and teapot.

Oh, great, I thought as I fetched cups and saucers. Who the heck knew who *Thee* was? Blessèd sister of rivers and whatnot—ah, the poem's ending was a gorgeously worded disappointment. Nonetheless, when I reread "Ash Wednesday" at home on my own (Nell lent me her copy), I found myself fervently sharing one of the wishes voiced by the poem's speaker: *that I may forget / These matters that with myself I too much discuss.* Yes, I thought, why not just cancel all this existential difficulty, turn away from it . . .

But could I really do that?

Doubtful, I consoled myself with another pair of lines, each offering not an idea but an image: *Rose of memory / Rose of forgetfulness.* Two roses, each representing a basic human impulse: to retain, to let go.

I'd pick each rose, I decided. I would learn to do both things. Yet memory and forgetfulness constituted *one* rose, the poem said. *The single Rose.* How could that be? I envisioned a single blossom with variegated colors, drenched and lovely as a sunset's. Very nice; but as the rest of the stanza revealed, the situation was complicated. Apparently this single rose wasn't just a blossom encompassing both recollection and obliviousness; it was something more. It was *the Garden / Where all loves end.*

I contemplated this.

So the single rose was a garden, and in this garden all loves end. All right, I thought—all right, Eliot. But only if in this poem *end* meant *wind up* and not *terminate*. Or *arrive* and not *stop*.

The more I thought about it, the more uncertain those alternative meanings left me. Was it possible that remembering and forgetting were *both* where love goes to ground? And could this be neither good nor bad, neither positive or negative, simply ineffable?

Indeed it could. Indeed it was.

Conclusion of all that / Is inconclusible: those lines from "Ash Wednesday" baffled me then, but come clear to me now. They conjure my father, spading his mother into her garden.

I sometimes miss Nell fiercely, and am glad that on this day of brisk capricious winds and fast-running clouds, their shapes rippling like the Delaware's waters, she has visited me here in Castiglione. (*In spirit*, as she'd have said—a phrase connecting usefully with the verb *inspire*, from the Latin: to breathe or blow into.)

My grandmother gave me what her daughter-in-law never could, for my mother would deem it a waste of time: permission to make a mess, to get it all wrong, and a lesson in the need to clean up after—or at least make a good-faith effort to do so. I'd like to think that between these two women, my mother and my grandmother, I've got my bases more or less covered. But that presupposes I'll recognize my demons when they knock, and bar the door to them—and who can count on that?

8. *Casino*

THE PATH OPENS OUT ONTO A GRANITE BLUFF OVERLOOKING
the north end of Giglio Porto, the island's port.

It's early September, and Antonio and I are on the island
of Giglio for a week's stay. This isn't our first time here; every
summer since 2008, we've briefly rented the same small apartment. Located just outside the walls of Giglio Castello, a quiet
medieval *borgo* perched atop one of the island's highest hills,
the apartment is perfect for work and rest. When I stand on
its terrace, with one left-to-right, 180-degree glance I can take
in Castello up above and then—out in the dazzling waters—
the Argentario peninsula off the mainland, the small island of
Giannutri nearby, and (on very clear days) far-off Monte Cristo
and Elba.

Standing on the bluff, I stare at the strangeness before
me. A few hundred yards to the left of the breakwater lies the

half-submerged carcass of a boat. Longer than the entire town's width, it is blue and white and multi-decked and funneled. I cannot help but see it as a child's bath toy whose proportions somebody got grotesquely wrong. Houses a few hundred feet from the carcass look miniature in comparison to it.

In the water nearby stands a sentinel, a high navy-blue crane. Lights are strung on it and on the carcass, just above the waterline; their reflections shimmer unsteadily on the surface of the sea. Like Lilliputians, men move on the rocks and on the deck of a barge alongside the carcass. I cannot see them from here, but I know what they look like: they wear orange or red jumpsuits, rubber boots, and hard hats. Perhaps a few wet-suited divers are in the water as well. A small boat is moored near the crane; it ferries the Lilliputians back and forth.

From where I stand, I can't hear anything but the wind. Down by the carcass, the slap-and-shush of the water and the undulating murmur of the trees compete with the all-day, all-night drone of heavy equipment. The mainland is to my left; to the right, westward, the sea appears infinite, the horizon merely an idea—unevenly visible, at times indistinct.

Earlier, I watched a squall travel across the peninsula, an hour's ferry ride from here. For a few minutes, air and water alike turned an ever-deeper gray, their tones merging; then a rectangle of sky cleared right at the horizon. It was as if a theater director had decided to part the curtains of rain so I could glimpse what lay on some lit-up stage behind the one spread before me. I stood watching, convinced the world was letting me in on a fundamental secret of its drama, its mysterious workings. I was a spectator without a *chiave di lettura*, the right way to perceive what I was looking at.

Quietly majestic for a few moments, the scene's lighting gradually dimmed. Then the curtain dropped, and all returned to a uniform gray.

The *Costa Concordia*, a Costa Crociere vessel, was launched in 2005 at a cost of roughly $570 million. Designed to accommodate more than four thousand people (a quarter of them crew members), it is slightly over 950 feet long and 116 feet wide. The boat has thirteen public decks on which are approximately 1,500 cabins.

The *Concordia* has four swimming pools (two with retractable roofs), five Jacuzzis, and a poolside movie theater on the main pool deck. There are five onboard restaurants, thirteen bars, and numerous "entertainment options," including a three-level theater, a casino, and a disco. A children's area is equipped with video games. For those who wish, the boat also has a Grand Prix racing simulator. Needless to say, there's an Internet café.

One could say the *Concordia* is a floating island for people of leisure. One could also compare it to a quarantine center for individuals with a particular pathology: they want to be distracted, they enjoy encountering thousands of people daily, and they love the notion of a sea voyage but don't want to be too aware of water. Such is sea-cruising in the early twenty-first century: passengers do on boats all the things they do on land and none of the things they might do at sea.

Shortly before 10:00 p.m. on the evening of January 13, 2012, the *Concordia* hit a submerged rock off the coast of Giglio, a small island in the Tyrrhenian Sea roughly ten miles from the Tuscan coast. The rock was very near Le Scole, a visible cluster marked on navigation charts.

The submerged rock put a long gash in the boat's side. The *Concordia*'s lights went out; plates and glasses fell from dining tables. Passengers were told only that power had been lost, not that the boat had struck a rock and was taking on water. The *Concordia* soon rotated and drifted to shore at the edge of Giglio Porto. Brought to a halt there, the vessel listed heavily, its bow and stern held up by two large ledges of rock. Having thus foundered, the *Concordia* was left—many say abandoned—by its captain, Francesco Schettino, who went to land while his crew continued loading people onto lifeboats.

Some passengers swam the few hundred feet to the coast, managing to do so because the water was mercifully serene, the moon full, and the wind low. Others were rescued by helicopter. Most were taken ashore either in lifeboats or by Gigliese motorboat owners. The evacuation of the *Concordia* was a chaotic operation; its crew seemed not to have been prepared for anything remotely like such an event.

Nonetheless, in roughly four hours the boat was evacuated. This meant that more than four times the total of Giglio's full-time population of nine hundred souls was all at once deposited in its little port.

The evacuees climbed out of lifeboats and small craft in casual and evening dress, in gym clothes and bedclothes. Many were shoeless, and quite a few were scraped and bruised; a few had broken bones and serious cuts, having fallen against and upon one another in precipitous descents from decks to small boats. Most were composed but frightened, confused, and distressed. Some, lacking any idea where they were, wanted to know where the nearest airport was.

Thirty-two people failed to make it to shore alive. Eight months later, two bodies have yet to be recovered.

Before the *Concordia*'s encounter with the rock, Captain Schettino had ordered the boat to pass by the coast of Giglio at a much closer distance and greater speed—sixteen knots—than are allowed.

His reckless act wasn't a one-time-only occurrence. Costa Crociere cruise ships were known for taking an *inchino*, or "bow," while passing Giglio, Procida, Ischia, and other Italian islands in the Mediterranean—drawing close enough that passengers and islanders could see, hear, and wave to one another. Weeks after his boat foundered, the *Concordia*'s captain said he'd sought to fulfill a promise to his chief of restaurant services, a Gigliese: the boat would pass close by the island so he could greet his family.

Shortly before the impact, Schettino was eating dinner. After the hit he called an onshore crisis coordinator several times, but he did not issue the abandon-ship order until seventy-four minutes after the ship ran into the rock. At some point during the evacuation, he boarded a lifeboat along with his second mate, and went to a rocky part of the shore close to the boat. An audio recording of his cell-phone call from there to a supervisor at the coast guard in Livorno soon went viral on the Web. The supervisor was clearly stunned to hear that the *Concordia* was going down while its captain stood on *terra ferma*, watching his remaining passengers and crew disembark.

Since the disaster Schettino has come under harsh attack, but he also has fervent defenders. Getting back on the boat, the latter claim, would've been impossible. Schettino himself has stated that despite having left, he managed the evacuation just as he would've done if he'd been aboard: by phone. The question of whether he could or should have returned to the boat will be addressed during legal proceedings. Meanwhile, Schettino is under house arrest, his maritime career over.

From our terrace, my view of the boat is such that it takes me a few moments to reckon with its actual proportions. I can grasp how long it is, but not how high. From Giglio Porto, viewers see it from a different angle, one that foreshortens it but makes it look much higher. From Castello, it looks nearly flat.

Antonio and I park our laptops on the kitchen table, where it's cool during the afternoon heat and light-filled all day. This week will, we've heard, bring clouds and a bit of rain, but we don't mind. Giglio's not a fancy or costly place to vacation, and for us, it's a little gem, sparkly and peaceful at once. The apartment's kitchen is right off the terrace, where we take brief work breaks to stretch our arms and legs.

But now there's the boat.

Each day I look at the *Costa Concordia* multiple times: first thing in the morning, last thing at night, and from various vantage points in between. Yet it's fruitless: I can't really grasp what I'm looking at. As it happens, the terrace's height above sea level is almost the same as the length of the *Concordia*. If the boat were turned head-to-tail so its prow were balanced on the water's surface, I'd be staring straight at the tip of its stern.

Giglio has a mere seventeen miles of coast. Much of the island is an uninhabited nature reserve, and most of its residents, full-time and visiting, live in three villages: Porto, Castello, and Campese. A few luxurious villas are tucked away in hard-to-reach spots, but there's no high-end entertainment or shopping on the island. In the summer months, the island's population swells with the influx of renters, campers, and time-share folk. Yet this isn't a heavily trafficked place; the number of ferries and cars is limited, and in any case there's little to do on Giglio other than eat, drink, and relish what nature offers.

I have rambled the island's paths and hiked steep stony trails, passed languid afternoons on little beaches at Arenella, Canelle, and Campese, strolled the length of Porto's main dockside street, and clambered up and down the narrow alleys of Castello. Though there's much I haven't explored, the island's vegetation and topography have become familiar to me. What

I mainly know of Giglio, however, is its mutability. It is impossible for me to fix in memory anything I experience here—the island's views or scents, the touch of its air and wind, the soughing of trees, braying of donkeys, flitting of birds' wings. Each year I arrive expecting I'll remember precisely how it felt the year before—physical sensations, Giglio's sensory imprints on my body—and each time, it all feels subtly different. Certain changes are obvious, of course: a new building in Porto, a favorite shop in Giglio Castello now closed. But such things happen anywhere. What's unusual, even uncanny, is the way this island seems to rebuff my efforts to capture and store it in my mind so when I return, the sensations I'm anticipating will match with what I'll feel.

This isn't just an annual challenge; it's a daily one. Stepping onto the terrace each morning, I'm startled by how unlike yesterday and unpredictive of tomorrow this here-and-now is. Why so, I wonder, on this island, when on the other island I call home—Brooklyn—all seems steadily fixed in reality and memory alike, and *this is how things are* remains a phrase I can utter unhesitatingly?

Perhaps for those Gigliese who awakened to the sight of the *Concordia* on that January morning, a similar perplexity arose as the familiar suddenly turned foreign. Worse: *how things are* had overnight become *what should never be*. For me, the experience of this island's unpredictability has always carried a positive charge. But I don't have to deal with a shipwreck that's unfolding in slow motion, the full extent of its consequences still to be reckoned with.

* * *

To reach open water from the tiny beach at Arenella, swimmers must either wade out over a bed of small rocks or take a less direct but more comfortable route between two large rock clusters at the southern end of the beach. A path of pale sand threads between the rocks; one must sidle carefully past them and then plunge in.

The plunge can't be too deep, however, as the water's still fairly shallow at that point. And once launched, swimmers must be attentive: there's another rock, flat and broad, just below the surface about ten yards from the beach. I've skinned my hands and knees on it more than once; it always seems to creep up on me, rather than the other way around.

This year—the year of the boat, as people say—I find that rock more compelling than nervous-making. I swim near it, circling it, trying to gauge its full dimensions. It sometimes seems like a sea creature, perhaps a huge turtle with a smooth hard back. I wonder what it'd do to one of the paddleboats that kids like to rent for an hour's spin. If such a boat's Plexiglas hull was to scrape against it, could the rock gash it open? Or could a paddleboat get hung up on the rock, stuck there, broiling in the sun? And could I myself climb upon the rock, since at its highest point it lies only six inches or so below the water's surface?

Just around an outcropping to the right of the beach at Arenella lies the carcass. One can't see the *Concordia* from the beach or cove, only the crane that towers above it. The outcropping blocks the view. Swimming out a few hundred feet, I lie on my back in the water and catch glimpses of the crane as I drift. In my mind I envision Gulliver, beached and inert, swarmed by rope-dancing Lilliputians.

There's a plan for the boat's salvage, a complex scheme that involves much pumping of air and water. The operation is fraught with difficulty and risks, both to the workers and to the environment. The Lilliputians' lights glow day and night as generators and heavy equipment run nonstop, making a relentless noise that can be heard intermittently even in Castello.

I find it hard not to admire such efforts. Still, as everyone on Giglio knows, with the right combination of unpredictable factors—winds and the water's action—the *Concordia* could drop out of sight altogether, leaving behind millions of dollars in equipment and five hundred workers.

It's really tricky work, say specialists on *Concordia*-related websites. No, it's a *mucca*, the woman who owns our apartment said to me during a conversation yesterday. (She lives in the house directly below ours, sharing our view.) The *Concordia*'s nothing but a cash cow for the salvage companies—and meanwhile, each morning I get up and step onto my terrace and look and . . .

Her voice trailed off. She made a stabbing motion at her heart.

My thoughts go to the two victims whose bodies have yet to be found: an Indian musician and a Sicilian woman.

Did they try to leave but fail for reasons no one, including themselves, could ever know? Or did the whole thing—the impact, the drift toward shore, the increasing list of each deck— catch them totally unawares, unable to react fast enough? Were they napping when it all began? Listening to music with headphones? Or did they attempt to get off the boat in the company of others who, fleeing, weren't capable of helping them, or figured they were following right behind, or believed someone else was with them, making sure they'd be all right?

Then I think about the survivors. More than 4,200 people who, a few hours before the encounter with the rock, had dined in one of the *Concordia*'s restaurants, or played a game of tennis, or indulged in a Jacuzzi session, or had their hair or nails done, or seen a film, or listened to live music as they were conveyed toward the coast of a little island off Tuscany that they'd never heard of—all these passengers who, post-encounter, wandered in a daze through a town with two main streets, a church, a few hotels, a dozen or so places to eat and drink, some shops selling trinkets and sweatshirts and local wine, a couple of touring agencies and real estate offices, a butcher, several ice-cream shops, and a small exhibit room of a man who makes wonderfully detailed models of boats . . .

What did those survivors take away from their few hours in Giglio Porto—what sensations? Will their memories blur or cancel what happened between the moment of impact and their return to safe ground? What does the human body retain and recall of such phenomena as a cruise ship bowing to a coastline, bumping into a rock, tipping over, then glub-glubbing to one side while thousands of people scramble to get off it?

In Porto, shopkeepers and merchants have had a virtual double season of work since mid-January. The port has been housing and feeding journalists, salvage workers, and thousands more day-trippers than would normally arrive, particularly during the late-winter and spring months. Touring boats of all kinds have come from as far as Elba and Corsica. Full-time Gigliese admit to feeling exhausted by the voyeurism of tourists who don't bother to visit Castello or explore the island's natural beauty.

All the actors in this drama have their own perspectives and needs, fears and fantasies. And everyone has a story to tell about it, though not everyone is willing or eager to do so. On the website of Carnival (Crociere's parent company), the keywords "Costa Concordia" produce nothing: it's as if the vessel never existed, was never associated with Carnival. On Costa Crociere's news blog, in contrast, the story line is tightly controlled: *We are now launching a salvage operation with characteristics and technical complexities never faced before.* An accompanying video shows a massive white cruise ship sunning itself on its side, propped up by a splendid Mediterranean island and looking like some magnificent bauble in paradise.

As the story of the disaster keeps unfolding, there will be alliances and negotiations, winners and losers. In Italian, the somewhat vulgar slang for a big fat mess is *casino.* The Italian word doesn't refer to gambling; a *casino* is a whorehouse. When

I combine the word's meanings in both languages—brothel and betting-place—I find a useful (if partial) *chiave di lettura*. From start to finish, the *Concordia* has been a *casino*.

Yesterday afternoon, to get a closer view, we descended by car from Castello to the turnoff to Arenella, and parked on the narrow road's even narrower shoulder.

A little gap had opened in the guardrail. We slipped through on foot and started downward over rocks till we could go no further—too steep, too dangerous. We were smack in front of the *Concordia*, a few hundred feet as the crow flies. I sat down and scanned the length of the boat with my binoculars, trying to memorize what I was seeing.

A tangle of deck chairs above the largest of the swimming pools. Nearby, many more chairs (each tan with a silver rim) neatly stacked in rows; elegant, made to last. At one end of each pool, a pair of large planters in which, heads bowed, are palm trees whose fronds are brown. A bright-yellow swath around the perimeter of the top deck, its two ends disappearing into water: the jogging track. Staircases: several, each steep. (So many decks underwater! Less than half the boat is now above the surface.)

Countless windows, nothing inside visible. A tennis court. The retractable glass roofs of atrium-style restaurants or lounges.

Putting down the binoculars, I adjusted my seat on a rock, digging in with my sneakers so as not to slip downward. My vision unassisted, I found that my sense of proportion was once again boggled by what lay before me. The vast cruise ship;

a floating barge with a crane and other equipment; a second floating platform with stacks of storage containers; a tugboat; a powerboat. I studied the powerboat, minuscule in comparison with the *Concordia*. On it were a half-dozen or so figures resembling dolls. I raised the binoculars so I could watch them. They were dressed in white, whereas the men on the platforms were in red or orange jumpsuits. Then I gazed at the tugboat, where I could see laundry drying and more men moving about.

If any of those workers were to look up, I thought, they'd see the *Concordia*'s decks towering over them at a radical slant. Like the Leaning Tower of Pisa. They'd be staring upward as they pictured themselves on the boat's uppermost deck—up there, way way up, then starting to slide down, down down down . . .

It's throwing off our sense of proportion, said Mattia Carfagna when we called him a few days after the event. We're having trouble getting used to it, he added. We round a corner and there's the boat, and nothing seems the proper size.

Mattia runs a *ristorantino* in Castello that serves fish dishes. We met him last year, and were charmed by his humor and impressed by his talent. He knows Giglio and its people intimately; knows, too, the pleasure of time passing at its own pace on this island where nobody rushes, yet things get done.

Shortly before eleven on the night of January 13, Mattia went down to Porto and, along with dozens of fellow Gigliese, did what needed doing—bringing evacuees up to Castello in search of friends or relatives, and carting equipment and food from his restaurant down to Porto in order to make meals and hot drinks. It was cold, he recounted, there were so many people, wet, hungry . . . We didn't stop till two o'clock the next day. We were pretty much in a daze the whole time, even though we were well organized. It all felt . . . distorted.

When we saw Mattia for the first time after the disaster, Giglio's weather had turned cool—unusual for early September, though nothing like that January night. Mattia invited us to sit at the counter at the back of his restaurant; he was prepping food for that evening.

Here, he said, pulling out some *culatello* and *Parmigiano*. Eat this, warm up, have some wine while I work.

He put meat, cheese, bread, and wine before us, and we did as he instructed—ate and drank—and didn't ask about the boat. It was clear from his grimace, when I mentioned it in passing, that he didn't want to talk about what'd happened. Yet in the end he did, if only briefly. How not? The *Concordia* refuses to be silenced, though the boat doesn't speak.

I just want it, said Mattia, to go away. All of it.

From our terrace I can't see the Lilliputians at work. Can see only the sweep of the sea, the silvered tips of shrubs, pale lichen on crags below me. Can see, if I position myself right—turned, that is, away from the boat—only what I wish to see: Giglio's vertiginous hills, its high broad sky and mutating clouds. The island's serrated edges, where rock cuts into sea.

This place is one big rock, I remind myself. It can't drift off, crash, or get split open like a coconut because somebody's not paying attention. It's not a vessel. It won't sink.

Staring out across the Mediterranean, I travel mentally to the cemetery down the hill from Castiglione, with its little colony of graves and a mangy cat for a caretaker. From there, my mind leapfrogs to my parents' residence outside Philadelphia. Closing my eyes, inhaling deeply, I see my mother sitting next to me on the terrace—not the one in the *borgo*, not the one where she lives, but this terrace here on this island . . . No, that's not right, it can't be, for my mother *ranges where no one can see*—isn't that her bobbing out there in the Mediterranean, right now?—my mother, who must've felt split open like a coconut when told she'd soon cease seeing her husband, children, and everything else?

I open my eyes. The sea is placid; on its surface nothing moves but two ferries, one bound for Giglio and the other for the mainland. Where my mother ranges is a mystery. Swimming for decades in darkness, making her own light within herself because she alone can know what the experience was and still is—after all that, I bet Mom's truly tired, *not waving but drowning* . . . And has there really been nothing else I could've done about it, to help her—nothing other than love her? What's more, in recent years haven't I failed her by not doing what matters to *me*—my work—every day, trusting myself as she trusts me to weave words daily, sending that shuttle back and forth even if I can't see how it'll turn out, or if it'll be any good? Haven't I disappointed her? I've no kids and no new book, either, since quite a few years . . .

Anguish rams my heart.

Stop it, I order myself. You'll come back here in a few years, and when you return, you'll pretend the nightmare of the boat never happened. By then the boat will be gone. You'll sit at the table in the apartment and do your work, just as you sit at your desk in Castiglione or in Brooklyn and do it there. And you'll pretend Mom's still alive, even if she's not. If she's dead, then each afternoon you'll take a break from your work and go down to Arenella and swim out past the rock, out to where the boat used to be, and you'll stop and float, closing your eyes as tightly as they're closed right now, and with that absence of light you'll see what you need to see: the wispy curls of Mom's white hair, the perfect ovals of her fingernails, the soft lobes of her ears. In the waves' rise and fall you'll hear the upturn of her voice, that lilt when she teases you. Lapped by the water as you float, you'll feel Mom's fingers scanning your face, reading what you look like now. And all this will buoy you.

Oh yes, answers my heart. You'll swim out there, of course. And you'll remember. But don't forget what Eliot said about it, *the ragged rock in the restless waters*—how that rock is useful for steering a course, how fog hides it, waves slosh over it; how on calm days it's just a harmless monument to torments past, gone, over. But when the weather changes, *in the sombre season or the sudden fury*, that rock turns real, *is what it always was*. Memories that buoy will gash, too. Don't try guessing when or where.

* * *

How will Mattia and all the other Gigliese feel when the boat's gone, one way or another? Will they miss its presence, perverse though that possibility might sound to them now?

Perhaps they will wonder why they can't seem to summon the *Concordia* clearly to mind. Do things sink in memory? Under what circumstances does memory salvage disasters, or bury them? Will the islanders seek a *chiave di lettura* for their experience, or will they consign the *naufragio* to legend—like the Saracens' attacks four hundred years ago, which their predecessors bravely repelled, though who thinks about any of that today?

At dusk, the boat's an amusement-park ride gone topsy-turvy.

Midday, a tipped-over toy in brilliant sunshine.

At sunset, a blue-and-yellow hallucination.

Middle of the night, a huge dark blotch of sorrow.

First thing in the morning, a reminder: this will alter, will not be recalled as it is.

9. The Trunk

We've left Castiglione del Terziere for a fortnight—our second departure since moving there in late spring. It's autumn now; the island of Giglio and its boat are far away. Time and place seem out of whack, though of course the problem isn't time and place but my perception of them, distorted by travel.

And, too, by strong feeling.

We're in the States: we've come to visit my parents. On this mild fall morning, we've taken a train from New York to Philly, and have hopped a taxi outside 30th Street Station. In twenty minutes we'll arrive . . .

Six full days in an assisted-living community—what was I imagining when I made this plan? Me at the tender age of fifty-seven, and Antonio a mere sixty-five?

* * *

The place is kind of nice, actually.

Its residents call it a campus, as if it were a school. From the main building several hallways, all wheelchair-accessible, radiate into corridors of apartments on two levels. In spring, forsythia and azaleas blaze gold and pink; each autumn, old-growth trees litter the ground with burnt-orange leaves. A walking path encircles the grounds, wending through a patch of woods. The entire ensemble is tranquil; the only sounds one hears are those of lawnmowers and leaf-blowers. Birds feast at well-stocked feeders.

Settling into the cab, I picture the facility's main dining room, where we'll soon eat lunch with my parents. It's got a vaulted ceiling and a ski-chalet-style fireplace. Along the main corridor leading to the dining room is an exhibit space for residents' artwork: drawings, oils, watercolors, photographs.

After her heart attack, my mother was moved from Dad's apartment to the facility's nursing wing, called the Lodge. Dad walks over there several times daily to spend time with her. Along the way, he chats people up. Though I can't imagine not getting irritated by my father's repeated jokes—a by-product of his dementia—the maintenance men he greets each day always chuckle when he delivers one of his punch lines as if for the first time.

As a radio operator during World War II, Dad was stationed in China. He still talks incessantly about his wartime experiences, and loves trotting out the few Chinese words he can remember. He's even taught a couple of the staff to repeat *ding hao* and *bu hao* (*very good* and *not good*) when he barks out those phrases. It's touching to see how obliging the staff are: they play the game without impatience.

And yet, I remind myself as our taxi speeds along the Schuylkill Expressway, none of them have to worry about what's likely to come: that moment when my father can't recall who he's talking to, or know what he's trying to say.

This worry belongs mainly to my siblings and me. In fact, Dad has already started to fumble his words, mixing up phrases and parts of speech. When syntactical patterns escape or fail him, he tries others to see if they'll fit. Observing this, I'm reminded of my own end runs when speaking Italian—moments when I can't find what I need to complete a thought, and must scramble for rearrangements.

Look, says Antonio, pointing. Just like the ones on the Po River!

We're passing Boathouse Row. My husband cranes his neck to track a half-dozen racing shells slicing the water. I know what he's doing: focusing on something—anything—that'll take his mind off our destination.

Only a week, I repeat like a mantra as our taxi pulls up to the main entrance of the facility. Just a week. Then Antonio and I will fly back to our *borgo*.

We go to my mother first, wheeling our luggage over to the Lodge and down several hallways smelling more than faintly of poop and vomit. A few of the residents here are able to push walkers; most are in wheelchairs or propped up in bed, televisions on high volume.

My mother's room is near a terrace at the end of a hall, hence quieter and brighter than most. Its sunshine is helpful not to her but to my father, who can't abide gray or cold weather and is happiest in overheated spaces. He wears several layers even in summer; the slightest breeze provokes his complaints about the cold. Entering Mom's room, we slip off our jackets and park our luggage along one wall.

My mother sits in her easy chair, her back to the picture window. She's holding her audio player on her lap. An old, boxy plastic device she's had for years, the machine plays audio-books, called Talking Books, which are loaned by the Library for the Blind to visually impaired patrons. Mom's audio player is always either on her lap or at her feet. Several of the Library's bright green cassette containers rest by her hip: she's probably about to finish one title and start another.

Her expression is pensive; she's engrossed. The voice reading the book (quite loudly, so she can hear) is male, with a slight British accent. A room of some sort is being described, there's a detail about wallpaper . . . As she listens, my mother's eyeballs stray back and forth, as they've done for years.

Shifting my gaze from her face to her body, I see one of her hands travel to the waistband of her sweater, giving it a little tug and twist.

Each morning, a nurse dresses Mom. Today she's wearing an incongruous mix: a pink mohair pullover, heavy brown sweat-pants, and green-and-black floral-print socks with sneakers. Around her neck is a long, thin gold necklace, its three strands twisted together. The necklace is, I'm sure, the sole thing my mother herself chose to wear today. I helped her buy it in Boston, many years ago. Seeing it twinkle now in the sunlight, I flash onto a memory of that summer afternoon: Mom in a jewelry shop, fingering various lengths of gold, asking me to describe each one precisely before settling on the necklace she'd buy—among the least expensive, yet lovely.

In her sense of style, my mother has always managed an effortless polish. Frugal by nature, she used to sew her own skirts and dresses when she was young, using Vogue patterns. As she lost her sight, her tactile sense strengthened; over the decades, she's put her hands to work in all kinds of ways—playing piano, knitting and weaving, gardening, making ceramics. Her fingers feel and judge the qualities of fabric, leather, and clay. A visit from me rarely passes without her asking me to take off my shoes so she can feel them.

No doubt the peculiar outfit she's wearing today would make her moan in embarrassment, if she could see it.

Antonio and I glance at one another. There's no point announcing our presence to Mom; her Talking Book is too loud for her to hear us.

I move toward her. When I place my hand on her forearm, she starts a little—I've broken the spell. Then she lays a hand on mine, running her fingers over my knuckles, reading texture and shape: Is this person a nurse? A social worker? I keep my hand still. She takes note of my rings, an interlocked pair with an amethyst and a moonstone. Smoothing each stone with a fingertip, she breaks into a grin of recognition.

Ah, she says, turning off her tape recorder. It's you! You're here! *Good!*

Yes, I say, it's me—and Antonio, too . . .

I lean over and wrap my arms around her. She smells of institutional soap; the scent isn't unpleasant, but it's not hers. As I embrace her, she puts her hands on my head and tousles my hair.

Shorter than usual? she asks brightly. Her fingers trot across my shoulders and down my sides, then return to my head, re-investigating my haircut.

My wife's hair is beautiful, Antonio intervenes. Really!

Molto bello? asks Mom, showing off her minimal Italian.

Sí, molto! I love it short!

That's what counts, she says, smiling at Antonio's gallantry.

Hey, I inject in mock offense, shaking her shoulder lightly. What about me?

Oh, she says, I do care what you think about your hair . . . but your husband's opinion is more interesting.

She doesn't mean this literally; it's a classic Mom statement, snarky but not. It's affection in disguise. Antonio laughs. I've never had to do any translating for them: they know how to read one another.

Dad enters the room. His *oh!* of happy surprise—he's clearly forgotten we'd be arriving today—drowns out whatever Mom's saying. Taking her hand, I squeeze it lightly. I can feel how she's aged. It's harder to track deterioration when visits with her are only four weeks apart. But I've been away for over four months, and the changes show. Her body is slack, a little more stoop-shouldered than it was.

Dad moves to embrace me. Under my palms his back feels bony; he's lost some weight. Hi, darlin', he says. Oh, we're so glad you're here!

Yes, says Mom softly. Yes. It's been a while.

I know this is as close to *I've missed you* as she'll get. But speaking those words myself isn't—not yet—what I can do. We're alike, she and I: when reuniting, we don't effuse. Confronted with evidence of her increased frailness, though, I feel unsure. Will our usual implicit *I know you know* be good enough? The situation has changed: I'm living abroad, she's got heart disease. Do she and I need to do things differently? And on whose behalf am I asking these questions—hers, or mine?

You know, Antonio says to my father, your daughter and I will be here for six whole days! Wow. I hope you realize we'll be the youngest residents . . . I'm a teenager, actually.

Hah, says Dad. A teenager with almost no hair? You're a baldy! Hey, who's your friend? he asks, grinning at me. Pointing one forefinger at Antonio, he uses the other to trace a *you're crazy* circle in the air around his ear.

Our days in the assisted-living community proceed at an uneven tempo. In this sense, they're very like our days in Castiglione.

Mornings move briskly: Antonio and I work on our translation project and leave Mom and Dad to their usual routines. Afternoons seem to dilate. Supper comes earlier than we're used to. Every other evening, we sit and chat with my parents while they eat at six o'clock, then say goodnight and head into town for a noninstitutional meal at eight or so. One night we stay up very late, reading; the next, we tumble into bed like an old couple and are asleep by ten. At four the following morning, I awaken to find that Antonio's eyes are open, too.

Is this lurching of time inevitable during a *caesura*, or simply a matter of chance here in Philly? Perhaps other factors impinge. On the island of Giglio, time seemed stalled because of the boat stuck on its side. Once the *Concordia*'s gone, will days on the island pass at a faster, steadier clip? Or will time sway uncertainly as it tries returning to an even keel? Didn't my own days seem to go faster, then slower, then faster in the weeks before and after Andrea's passing?

Antonio and I have a quiet room on the second floor of the guest house, as it's called. As it happens, we're the only guests all week. At breakfast, Antonio and I pad around the kitchen in our pajamas as if we own the place. I'm struck by how steady Antonio has been since our arrival; he's thrown himself uncomplainingly into the weirdness of being here, which helps make my sadness about my mother's decline easier to handle.

We check in with my parents before work. Dad's morning opens with a slow breakfast and NPR news, after which he does his five minutes on the treadmill, fetches the mail, and tinkers at his desk. My mother, too, listens to the news after taking her breakfast in the Lodge. Then she settles into a Talking Book for the rest of the morning.

These days, I've discovered, she's drawn mainly to thrillers and mysteries, which I've been phone-ordering for her from Italy.

She's keen on the novels of Alan Furst—noirish World War II narratives—and John le Carré's spy tales. She claims not to follow their plots, but I'm amazed at what she reports after reading them: in her retellings, the knots untie and the twists somehow make sense. She's alert to the characters' underlying motives and flaws.

I spend the latter part of every morning with her, before all four of us meet for lunch. Mom and I speak about what she's reading. About Antonio's son, daughter, and grandchild; about the translation project; about the cats in the *borgo*. About different types of risotto. About the elderly castle owner's impending death. My mother is interested in all of it, though dispassionate about *il professore*. If an afflicted person is over eighty years old, her reaction to news of his or her ill health is likely to be a shrug of the shoulders. When, on the third day of our visit, I tell her we don't know how much longer Bononi will be with us, my mother turns pointedly to practicalities.

What'll Raffaella do? she asks. My mother's always been good with names; I rarely have to introduce anyone in my stories more than once.

I dunno, I answer. Raffaella herself doesn't know. It's like Bononi's part of the castle itself, and nobody can imagine him not being there anymore.

He'll haunt it, then, Mom says. Isn't that what happens in castles?

My mother doesn't need to be told that it's tough when one's partner of many years is no longer present, there one day and gone the next. If Dad goes before her, I wonder (not for the first time), how will she fare?

She'll rally, I think. She'll make sure she's not too much alone.

Or will she? Might she not, instead, use the reality of solitude—not to mention blindness, hearing impairment, heart disease, arthritis—like a springboard, to launch herself more quickly across her own finish line? Might that not be her secret wish?

I don't know. Don't know, either, what I want for her, or for myself. Gazing at her now, I recall vividly what I used to sense, long ago, as she was going blind: that her self-possession was saving and endangering me at the same time. Back when I was still a child, it spared me her inevitable grief, fear, and anger; these she kept wholly to herself. Yet at the same time, her self-control pushed me into the vortex of those same feelings of my own, much as I longed to ignore them. Mom's management of the unfolding situation ensured that I'd never speak with her outright about what and how she was suffering, yet I could nonetheless imagine it. And react, and suffer as well. And, worse, feel ashamed for suffering.

By the way, Mom asks, have you found another of those undershirts at your local market? I love the one you sent me.

She's referring to a wool-and-silk tank top I mailed a month or so ago. It's practical and well-made, the sort of undergarment old ladies across Europe have worn for centuries. My mother is frequently cold, though she never used to be; she often used to wear short-sleeved shirts in winter. Now she's bundled in wool, and it's only October.

Ah, Ma, I say, you beat me to it! I wanted to surprise you . . . Actually, I've already snuck a couple in here. Two different types, for variety. I was planning on telling your nurses not to show them to you till after I leave.

Mom likes a good trick, especially if it involves accomplices.

Too late now, she says, smiling. Let me see.

It's usual, this phrasing of hers—*let me see*. Normally those words roll right off me. But I'm already primed for pain, so her phrase dunks me directly into the well. For years I've taken pleasure in buying clothes for my mother; it's something she didn't—couldn't—do for me when I was a teenager, and doing it for her now, I feel I'm setting things right. Of course I want her to see what I've brought her from Italy. But suddenly I want my mother to *see*—to see all, I mean, and right this instant: not just the two undershirts but Dad, my siblings and me, my husband, my siblings' families, and everyone and everything else Mom would want to see, plus all she doesn't even know exists, all that would thrill her if she were to lay eyes on it; and the ferocity of this wish makes my own eyes prick and leak.

Pulling one of the two undershirts from my knapsack, I blot my eyelids carefully with its hem, then unfold it neatly in her lap.

What color is it, she asks.

Cream, I said. They're both cream. That's the standard-issue color for this stuff in Italy, Mom.

I'm glad, she says. Cream goes with everything. I've never thought much of white undershirts.

Oh god, I say, tell that to Dad. All of *his* have turned gray.

Then do me a favor, she says. Go into his drawers, throw out every single one, and buy him a set of new ones. Three, at least. With V-necks, please. So he doesn't look like a truck driver when he wears a button-down shirt.

He'll know you put me up to it, Ma. He hates spending money on himself...

Don't worry, she responds, smiling. I'll manage him. D'you need my wallet? It's in the bottom drawer of the bedside table. I'm pretty sure there's a ten in it.

My mother doesn't realize that a three-pack of men's undershirts is likely to cost more than ten bucks. It's been a while since I've taken her across the road to the little mall where she used to enjoy a bit of shopping. She hasn't had the energy.

I watch as she passes her fingertips across the undershirt and around its armholes, assessing the fabric and cut. Giving the top a light shake, she traces its length. Finally, she returns her fingers to its neckline.

Very nice, she says. Toasty fabric, but not heavy. And it's got lace here, doesn't it? Around the neck.

Yep, I say. Cream-colored, of course.

Good. Your father will like the lace, she says.

As always, I'm moved by how my mother relies on her husband's appreciation of her looks, appearance, clothing. She's right: Dad *will* notice.

Now, says Mom, show me the other top.

My friend the poet Liam Rector used to assert, by way of a motto, *Nobody gets to stay.* As he wrote in one of his best poems, "Handmade Shoes," *going was Liam's / Real subject. He in fact / Thought of little else.*

Suicide was his response, five years ago, to the question of how to go. For him, "taking matters into one's own hands" wasn't a cliché but an imperative, the quid pro quo for existential freedom. *That boy paid / A price for living / The way he lived,* he wrote.

Liam's imperative, natural for him, has never spoken to my mother. Eye disease and hearing loss have extorted their price; she's used to paying it. The transaction doesn't bear on how she's chosen to live. For her, ending the whole shebang would be unseemly. I imagine my grandmother's suicide attempt still irks Mom—all that high-drama, in-the-bathtub bathos . . . Dad, however, is more susceptible to Liam's way of thinking. A few years back, realizing it'd be hard to acquire a sufficient quantity of the right kind of pills, my father somehow managed to procure a handgun for the purpose of eventual self-release. My mother made him get rid of the weapon as soon as he'd announced its purchase. (Ridiculous, she said. As if we need more reasons for gun control! And who gets to clean up after you? Dad ditched the gun.)

* * *

Sitting with her now in this sun-drenched room whose brightness she cannot perceive, I wonder what regrets my mother may harbor. Will any be passed along to me, an emotional legacy I may not be capable of resisting or refusing?

There's so much she might've done . . . In fact, Mom has consistently accomplished more than plenty of sighted folk. But that doesn't necessarily mean she has no regrets. And if she does, she's got no one to talk to about them—for sharing them with my father would be a lousy idea, as she surely knows.

So much she might've done . . . The phrase haunts my life, too. Admitting this to myself, I feel my throat constrict as if I'm about to choke. But now my mother's starting to take off her pullover; she wants to try on the second undershirt, and she'll need a hand getting that sweater over her head.

Clearing my throat (to me the noise sounds raw and imperative), I state loudly that it's almost time for lunch.

All right, she says. Help me out of this, please.

The task requires speed; she's clearly uncomfortable. I yank the pullover swiftly up her sides and over her head. My mother gives a little sigh of relief, and her shoulders sag. She's wearing a brassiere I bought her several years ago; it's faded and lumpy, ruined by high-heat spins in institutional dryers. Yet her unclothed torso retains its essential linear elegance; it doesn't appear to be that of a woman approaching ninety years old. I don't often see Mom half-dressed. The sight both moves and unnerves me.

Picking up her new undershirt, I ask her to raise her arms so I can slip it over her head. As she does so, I pull the top down carefully over her hands, elbows, head, and shoulders. Mom shimmies a little, letting the fabric settle on her. She gives the top a final downward tug.

Just right, she says. And I like the width of the straps, they're comfy. The trim—it's satin, isn't it?

You guessed it, I tell her.

She smiles, fingering the undershirt's neckline.

I pull a lightweight cardigan from her closet and help her put it on. I'm still thinking about the softly undulating folds of her torso. Having seen what my mother can't see—her body uncovered, her flesh—I'm feel as though I'm also seeing what I can't see: my mother's aloneness. The do-it-yourself-ness. The sovereignty, the solitude.

What else? I'm seeing my own self-doubt, which would fill my mother with impatience were she to know of it. So I keep it from her, just as I conceal the effects of the losses I've experienced. It's easy to imagine what she'd say if she knew: So your friends have died, you miss them—fine. But why have you made their deaths a prison and locked yourself into it? You're not going to do that with *my* death, are you?

Mom readies to stand up.

I take one of her hands in mine, pulling her lightly upward. She manages to get herself upright, wobbling a little. But can she stay that way?

Hold on, Mom, I tell her. I've got to wheel your chair around . . . Stay right where you are.

She sways as I let go of her hand, but doesn't topple. I've timed this wrong. Quickly, fearfully, I pull the wheelchair over and park it just behind her knees, locking its brakes. I should've brought the chair over before making her stand.

Okay. Are you ready, I ask.

Uh-huh, she says matter-of-factly. Just fine.

Reaching behind herself, she gropes for an arm of the wheelchair, grabs it with one hand, and drops into the seat, her frame torquing slightly as she descends. Her body lands with a thud.

Mom, I say. I missed you. I'm glad I'm here.

Me too, sweetheart, she replies, and it's not the words but her tone, unforced and unencumbered, which lets me know she really is fine. For now, at any rate.

Picking up her feet, she swings them adroitly onto the wheelchair's footrests. Then she places her hands firmly on the armrests. This is a daily ritual; she's done all these moves hundreds of times, with nurses I've never met. Some of the nurses must be even clumsier than I when it comes to wheelchair maneuvers. Then again, they spend more time with her.

Releasing the brake, I turn Mom around and wheel her toward the door.

And now . . . to lunch, she says. We don't want to keep those men waiting, do we?

* * *

The day before Antonio and I leave, a bit of drama shakes things up.

At lunchtime, Antonio finds me in the dining room as I'm pushing my mother toward the table where Dad is already seated. Their sandwiches—tuna, since today is Tuesday—await them.

Get her seated, Antonio says. I gotta talk to you for a moment.

At first I'm alarmed. Quickly rolling Mom up to the table, I excuse myself and return to my husband.

Don't worry, everything's okay, he says, smiling as he tugs me toward the salad bar. But you won't believe what just happened . . .

He recounts the incident as we fill our plates with greens. Because he needed to pick up a load of laundry down the hall, Antonio told my father to go ahead to lunch on his own. Then, returning to the apartment with the laundry basket, he carried the clean clothing into my father's bedroom and began sorting it. All at once he heard a sound and, assuming my father had come back for some reason, went to the kitchen.

There, standing before the fridge with his back to Antonio, stood a stranger in a parka. The fridge door was open. The man was chugging on a bottle of wine—a bottle my father kept chilled for my mother, so she could have a glass when she visited the apartment every Sunday afternoon. Hearing Antonio enter, the stranger started in surprise, wiped his mouth rapidly with the back of his hand, corked the bottle, and stuck it back in the fridge. Astonished, Antonio watched in silence as the man fled.

Can you remember what the guy looked like? I ask when Antonio finishes telling his story.

He was a resident, says Antonio. But it happened so fast . . .

Finding out who the man was necessitates some tact.

We can't, of course, recount to my parents what has just gone on in Dad's kitchen. Neither of them needs to be agitated. So I attempt an oblique approach, inquiring, while they (slowly, so slowly!) eat their sandwiches and fruit, about various residents. How's the nice lady who's always in the library, how's the cranky Republican? The conversation gradually works its way around to the man in the parka. Indeed, it's the parka's color, a vivid yellow, that allows my father to recall who he is.

Oh yeah, that guy, I know him, says Dad. Can't recall his name . . . Smart fellow. Lost his wife to Alzheimer's two years ago, poor guy. He was very committed to her. She was a tough patient, used to get kind of worked up, hard to manage. Anyway, he's a good man. But you know, I had to speak to him last year about something.

What, Antonio asks, and I carefully lay a hand on his knee under the table, warning him to stay impassive. My husband is quite capable of making a poker face, but I'm worried he'll start smiling. Or worse, chuckling.

Well, says my father, the guy used to come into the apartment when I wasn't there and drink my liquor. Now that I've stopped drinking—did you know I haven't had a drink in over a year?—

—yes, Dad, I break in, to spare us this repetition.

Well, I don't buy hard alcohol anymore, just some wine for your mother.

Not very good wine, inserts my mother teasingly.

Oh, I'll fix that for you, says Antonio.

Grazie, says my mother.

So anyway, says my father—wresting the narrative back so he won't lose track of it altogether—I don't buy liquor. But last year, there was still a half-full bottle of vodka in the cabinet, you know, the one in the kitchen? And this guy would come in and help himself to a shot of it now and then. Right out of the bottle! I caught him once or twice and told him, look, you shouldn't do this, you know. He was really embarrassed. I know he's had a hard time, but hell, you can't go around to other folks' apartments and drink their booze . . .

Poor guy, my mother says. I know she means it, but it's evident, too, that the story amuses her: she's half-smiling. Which gives my husband a reason to grin. Thankfully, my father doesn't notice; he's intent on wrangling a final piece of pineapple onto his spoon.

Who knows, Antonio says after we've seen my parents off to their afternoon naps. I mean, maybe the guy just enjoys the suspense. Like, will they catch me this time?

Ah, he must be so desperate, I say.

Or totally bored, says Antonio. Or really sad. Probably a mix. At least doing this thing he does, going from cabinet to cabinet—at least he stays alert . . .

True, I think. It could be worse: he could be sitting by himself in his apartment, swilling his own booze all day. Still, the image of him tippling his way down the hall unnerves me. I wonder how many other residents are more or less like this guy, superficially fine yet fundamentally desperate. And I picture Antonio and myself in fifteen or twenty years, assuming we stick around that long. An older couple, really truly older, and perhaps mismatched in health.

Mi strozzerebbe—Antonio would throttle you, I tell myself. He would, if he knew you were thinking this. So change the picture. Quick, revise!

I make myself imagine the two of us (old, yes, we're old) sitting on the wall of the church piazza in Castiglione. Legs dangling over; hands in our laps. A thick, bright blanket is wrapped around our shoulders. We're staring across the Magra Valley toward Aulla and the sea beyond. We don't talk, we gaze. Our minds are empty. The air in the piazza is never completely still; gentle now, the wind will pick up in a bit, we know. And when it does, it could tip us over. Sooner or later, in fact, we'll fall off the wall. But we're swaddled, so nothing will break.

Love-blanketed. Safe as a pair of babies.

After discussing whether to tell the staff about the incident with the liquor thief, we decide to leave it, and the drinker, alone.

The morning of our departure, Dad comes to us with news.

I've found a buyer for the Lincoln! he says. The head of maintenance here is a really good man, and he's got a college-age girl who needs a car. He'll take the Lincoln off my hands for a thousand bucks, which isn't bad, considering how many miles it's got! I've kept it in excellent shape, I have to say. That girl's gonna get a nice car from her dad.

He begins detailing his annual visits to the local mechanic. We've heard all this several times before, but we nod anyway.

So about the daughter of the maintenance fellow, I finally prompt my father. When will she take the car?

Oh, right. Next week, answers Dad. But you know, before I hand over the keys, I want to go to the car wash. Come on, he says, reaching for his coat. I'll show you how nice it looks!

We follow him to the parking lot. As he walks, my father lists slightly starboard; not like the *Concordia*, but he's not upright, either. At least he's still moving, unlike Mom, for whom each unsteady walk from chair to bathroom is a challenge.

There in front of the building sits Dad's beauty—black, long, and wide, a classic late-twentieth-century gas-guzzler. My father opens the driver's-side door, lowers himself in, and points out all the marvels: leather seats, a gleaming wood dashboard, electric windows, a radio that also plays tape cassettes. (Cars with CD players are well beyond his ken.)

A really great automobile, Antonio says as my father wraps up his tour of the car's interior. So well kept, too! We don't have anything like this in Italy. What a hit this car would be in our village . . .

Hearing this, my father breaks into his Italian-mafioso routine, Brooklyn accent and all. We've been treated to this performance of his before, on multiple occasions. He likes impersonating Lucky Luciano.

Today, though, Dad surprises us with a new variation. He pushes a button below the dashboard, and the car's trunk opens. Levering himself out of the driver's seat, he leads Antonio to the back and points at the opening.

Get in, he orders.

Antonio stares at him, unsure he's understood.

Turning to me, my father asks: Do you have your phone with you? It takes photos, right? I want you to document this! Okay now, Antonio—come on, hop in.

Dad, I say, are you serious?

Absolutely, he answers, grinning, and in that moment he reminds me of no one more than Antonio's grandson Milo, who at age three likes staging tableaux for us, with props of his own choosing.

My husband obliges.

He's not a basketball player, but he's not short, either. Yet remarkably, Antonio's lean frame fits into the trunk without much contorting. He lifts one leg up and into the trunk, plants his butt on the edge of it, and with a quick hop and roll, he's in. A bit of adjustment and he's prone in the clean, gray-carpeted space, hands folded behind his head and feet propped up. I'm seeing, as I do multiple times each day, what I so love about this man—his lightness of being, his lithe body, his grin.

Comodissimo, he says, settling in. Really! Good as a bed!

My father, miming the smoking of a fat cigar, launches into his "I'm-a-gonna-leave-you-in-cement-overshoes-in-the-river" monologue as I click away with my phone's camera. I'm happy: for a few moments my father and my husband have lost themselves in the drama of the Lincoln. Then Antonio, still smiling, climbs gracefully out of the trunk, and as Dad closes it, I feel my inner weather shift. Though the game we three have just played is as benign as a kindergartener's, I can't entirely set aside the sense that my husband was placed, if only for few minutes, in a kind of grave. He's fine, of course; it's the context that's spooking me. It's the bulletin board outside the dining hall with its list of recently deceased residents; it's the morbid odor permeating the Lodge; it's the booze-guzzler; it's the food no one really cares about, and why should they? It's all those hard-as-stone realities that people here confront daily.

They—we—all know what's coming. And yet *we row for years,* writes Donald Hall in his poem "Affirmation," *on the midsummer / pond, ignorant and content*—until upheavals large and small force us to affirm *that it is fitting / and delicious to lose everything.*

Delicious—really? Yes, because fitting. Because nobody gets to stay. Because, having affirmed this, we can still hop in a car trunk, take photos, and laugh. Because Mom will laugh at the scene, too, when I tell her about it. And I will make myself not think about her not seeing it.

Come on, love, says Antonio. Let's go with your dad to the car wash. Get in, Papá—no, in the passenger seat! I want to drive!

10. The Pass

THIS EVENING AFTER DINNER, A PHONE CALL ABOUT ONE OF Antonio's Cremonese relatives: an unanticipated, not-good medical diagnosis.

This afternoon, a lovely nap. In all innocence, as it were.

This morning, a three-hour drive up into the Appennini, the road often overhung by branches. Occasionally we crept past *frane*, little rockslides. As we crossed several narrow stone bridges over lush gorges—the bridges' parapets low and irregular, at points broken—I held my breath. The final bridge, just before the pass, was partially collapsed. Orange tape marked its usable lane. We crossed slowly, parked the car, and walked the length of the bridge's still-extant roadway, gazing down at a boulder-filled stream several hundred feet below.

Why, I wondered, wasn't the "safe" bit falling, too? Had the worst already happened, and we'd missed it this time?

Something else to guess at.

* * *

Earlier in the evening, before sunset, a walk up the hill from our village.

And a look back upon it, viewed from a neighbor's vineyard: the village's castle to the left, its square tower dominant; old stone houses spread along the main ridge of the *borgo*; and our little house-for-a-year, its terrace visible from "across the way," as my grandmother used to put it. Any stretch of space like this, over a leafy dell, was across the way to her.

Though no obvious bad illnesses dogged my grandmother, I've always believed she was an undiagnosed manic-depressive. There are days like today—sunshine brilliant, wind gentle— when I wish I had a soft version of Nell's illness instead of the one I've pegged myself as "suffering" (the word's not apt; "laboring under" is more like it): anxiety, the mind's habitual groove of disquiet. I awoke to it this morning, as I tend to do. Could feel it in my hand muscles' inadvertent twitching as the usual doubts about my work—my novel-in-progress—cycled through my mind and body. Today, could I not keep stopping to revise? Just keep going, simply be a writer and *write*? Saying goodbye to me a fortnight earlier, my mother urged me to finish my book. I could hear now the command beneath her encouragement: get it done!

Then Antonio rose, yanked the sheet playfully off me, and said, c'mon, *up!* Let's go to the Lagastrello Pass! We keep talking about doing that, and we still haven't . . .

Thus anxiety was transmuted into excitement as we ate breakfast, drove to nearby Monti, purchased two bottles of water, and began our ascent.

At first there was the town of Licciana Nardi. Then a handful of villages above it, sparsely populated. Then a few houses on their own, then fewer, then none—just hills—as the switchbacks commenced.

The roadbed got worse, the steepness serious. Around us were chestnut and hazelnut trees, intermittent stands of pine, and hardy wildflowers of all hues. The air was decidedly chilly. Above was a wide azure sky and multiform clusters of clouds. As we rounded one long curve, swerving midway for a *frana*'s deposit of crumbled rock, a dense swath of white materialized in the sky. It looked as though it'd been poured from a bucket—some painter's experiment in stippling gone extravagantly wrong.

More bridges, more curves. Then the bridge with the orange tape. Soon after, a sign announcing the summit of the pass. We were at two thousand feet or so, and decided to turn back rather than cresting the pass and descending to its other side, the Pianura Padana, Italy's flat agricultural "breadbasket" in the Po River valley.

Antonio patted our elderly car's dashboard in praise: what a climb you've just made! *Complimenti!* I, too, felt a giddy sense of achievement. We'd descended only a bit when, after a tight curve, the entire valley opened before us. Directly ahead, on a sloped field—gray upon green—lay some ruins, sun-drenched. We pulled over.

* * *

An old hospice, originally: so said the weathered sign.

Nearly a millennium had passed since the original structure, a stopping-off point for wayfarers and pilgrims, had first been constructed. Over the course of centuries, all manner of humans—traders and merchants, monks and adventurers, armies and partisans—had made their way to this edifice we were now reconstructing in our imaginations.

A safe haven, I said to Antonio. That's what we'd call a place like this, in English.

We stood gazing at broken walls dating from a couple of hundred years ago, not more. Stones from the older ruins were long buried, or had been carted away piece by piece. There was even an iron beam, evidence of a fairly modern attempt (and failure) at renovation. We saw a few lizards, some yellow buttercups in the grass. Listened to breeze and birdsong. The air smelled of nothing but itself.

I took a small triangular slab of rock from the site, prying it from the soil in which half of it was buried. Using my water bottle, I gave it a bath; it dried quickly. The slab would make a nice flat perch for something—a candle, maybe. And would remind us, I said to Antonio, of our day here. Of driving up-up-up to the pass.

As if I'd forget? I wouldn't. Still, I wanted the object, a tangible reminder. Just as, after her death, I'd wanted Nell's books, her watch, a few of her table linens. One Sunday back in the Seventies, setting the table for an Easter dinner at my grandmother's, I noted my mother, already seated, impatiently fingering a needlepoint ring that encircled her napkin. I figured Mom was distracting herself with something tactile—the better to tune out Nell's boasting, not for the first time, about her English family's sole link with royalty, some great-uncle who'd been a court photographer. Those same napkin rings, well over a century old, are with me now in Castiglione, a visual reminder of what I call FFFRs: fraught female familial relationships.

Antonio smiled at my little rock, then returned his gaze to the sloped fields before us. He had, as usual, no interest in hunting for mementos. He just wanted to take in the view.

I don't compulsively collect anything, mementos included. Yet in that instant I wished to be able to recall—always and readily, aided by the object in my hand—this nippy, bright, clean-aired day spent with my husband, both of us in good health. Glancing at him, I felt time split open: there stood Antonio in the here and now, and there he stood with Valeria many years earlier, one arm slung over her shoulder with that careless ease I could still easily conjure—their intimacy at once present and gone, real and over. And there stood Antonio and myself in Brooklyn, the autumn after Valeria's death, arms wrapped around each other, both of us astonished by a love so visceral and unexpected. By the renewal of body and heart, this fierce unstoppable flourishing. By its adjacency to loss.

A few years from now—five, ten, fifteen—would Antonio and I both be standing in Castiglione, basically fine? Or would he be taking care of me, as he'd taken care of Valeria during not one but two bouts of cancer? Or 1 of him? What new lessons in grief, what fresh trainings in loss would we have assimilated?

I felt my heart quietly spasm. There it was: *the torment of love unsatisfied*, as "Ash Wednesday" names it. And *the greater torment / of love satisfied*.

Do not resist, I told myself. Just let this be a wave, let it wash over you. *Even among these rocks*. Do not be afraid.

A few yards away from me, Antonio inclined his head back, relishing the sun. All I'd have to do, I knew, was turn to my husband and say *siamo fortunati*, and he'd look at me and guess what I was thinking. But I didn't want to break into his reverie; I could always tell him later, or keep it to myself. It didn't matter. Or did it? If I were to speak my fear, give it words, perhaps I'd corral it. Yet in doing so, I'd risk tugging Antonio from peacefulness to pain—and to what end?

My gaze returned to the small slab in my hand. I stared at it for a moment, then closed my eyes, pretending to be my blind mother: an old game played with myself. How would this thing feel to her?

Quite smooth, for a rock. Cool. Roughly triangular in shape.

The slab was part of this rocky redoubt, a place to which countless people before me had climbed. Travelers who'd seen the same green banquet spread before them; who'd forded the same streams wending down to the Magra and Taverone rivers; who'd had somewhere to get to, or someplace they needed to leave, or simply a sudden desire to explore the Lagastrello Pass... Why, I asked myself, was I retrieving from these ruins a piece of dove-gray rock rather than some other souvenir? A few wild-flowers, say, to press between a book's pages? Or an elegant pinecone, a piece of arty driftwood?

I couldn't say why. I simply sensed the little slab would call to mind the day's vibrancy. Would conjure that sense of possi-bility, of *don't be afraid, be glad*, that Antonio and I had felt as we crossed narrow bridges and skirted the *frane* in order to ascend and descend.

And, too, perhaps the slab would act like a poem, and offer a different reading of loss. I'd dug up this bit of rock for a reason, obscure though it might be; why not trust my impulse to unearth it? We humans are dog-like, after all; we excavate memories like bones, digging till we hit upon solace or some-thing close: a recognition that the dead don't wish it for us, this downward thrust of feeling. Want our faces upturned instead.

Antonio walked over to me, his expression calm and happy.

Pronti, amore? he asked quietly, taking my hand. You ready to return?

He kissed me, his lips warm. I reached up and stroked his head. We got back in the car and began wending our way down-ward, homeward. At Tavernelle, we deviated off the main road, then halted for a few minutes beyond Apella to give some don-keys the reign of the road. We stopped at last—thirsty, hungry—for lunch in Bagnone, a village a few bends of the road from ours. Nearly across the way.

* * *

Midday: a plate of simple pasta, a salad, and an espresso afterward, its almost-bitterness delicious.

Nighttime: an owl, its call reproving. Death, is it death you're dwelling on? *Hooo, hooo*—why, why? And Mia up at the castle, answering with her buoyant bark as if to say, oh, what do *you* know?

The small slab of rock sits now on a wooden chest in our living room. Where the slab comes from: a haven now in ruins. How it got there: carried by human hands. What it is: vestigial, a shard from a vanished whole. Which of my senses it most appeals to: touch, for its surface is nearly as smooth and cool as that of marble. How it serves, despite its indifference to time: as a base for a brass hourglass (whose, we'll never know) discovered at the bottom of a drawer.

11. *Libri*

WE'RE IN CARRARA, HAVING JUST VISITED THE NEAR-LUNAR landscape in the mountains above the city, where world-famous marble is excavated. Chilled to the bone, I'm willing the wee cup of espresso cradled in my hands to transmit its rich warmth quickly.

Up the street is the hospital where *il professore* died, several months ago.

I remember sitting by Bononi's bedside two days before his passing. He ranted a bit, then grew pensive and beautifully articulate, almost sweet. Then made a crude joke. Then ranted some more. The female nurses were alternately charmed and distressed by him. Perhaps he mistook them for past lovers.

Antonio and I held his hands. The skin of his chest was as smooth as a baby's. He was very pale, which made his light-blue-eyed gaze all the more intense. He spoke of going home, back to Castiglione, but we all knew—he did, too—that he wasn't.

* * *

Antonio chats with the barista as she prepares us another espresso. I stare into space, immobilized by the daze-making effects of our afternoon in the mountains. So much marble, such a vast whiteness! The sunlight spilling across the quarries was brilliant, almost blinding, and the air much colder than down in the city.

I stomp my feet lightly on the floor of the *caffè* to get the blood circulating. Into my head comes an e. e. cummings poem, the one that begins *Buffalo Bill 's / defunct* and then—in a tone of admiration larded with irreverence—tells of the legendary cowboy's prowess at shooting clay pigeons. The poem ends with a sardonic question: *how do you like your blueeyed boy / Mister Death.* There's no concluding question mark or period; the poem just abruptly stops.

Well, I think, Bononi with his blue eyes never rode *a water-smooth-silver stallion.* Yet in his own way, he, too, could shoot down *onetwothreefourfivepigeonsjustlikethat.* But no more.

I have a thing for Carrara marble. It is vivacious in appearance yet calming to the touch. Vulnerable to stains and scratches, it remains lustrous even when beat-up, desirable even if discolored. The men who quarry it, *i cavatori*, speak of it in tones of exhaustion and reverence. A great many local kitchen countertops and bathrooms are made of it, as are innumerable Lunigianese tombstones. Around here, if you want a good mortar and pestle, the right work surface for making bread, or a nice grave, you choose Carrara marble.

I touch it whenever I see it. Don't forget, it seems to say, the fate of the Roman city Luni, which once ruled our quarries . . . Nothing remains of that city now. Starting in the seventh century, Luni was attacked by Lombards, then by sea pirates, and later by an Andalusian emir—a freed slave and former high official of Córdoba's caliphate. Luni's residents fled to nearby Sarzana, never to return; and as the coastal plains on which it had been constructed gradually gave way to wetlands, Rome's once-prominent outpost disappeared. Still, the city does live on, as the lilting name of the region: *Luni*-gian-a. It has become music.

Standing in the hospital's *obitorio* with the other mourners, I didn't want to look at Bononi's body. So I concentrated instead on the marble floor. It was grayish white, its texture mottled and lustrous.

As we walked from the *obitorio* to the duomo where Bononi's coffin was transported for a memorial service, I saw marble everywhere. Carrara's main cathedral, reconstructed between the thirteenth and fourteenth centuries, has a soberly beautiful façade, striped with pale and dark layers of marble. Inside, mullioned windows let in daylight thin and pallid as creamy silk. Around a hundred of us filed in silently and took our seats on wooden pews. A priest from Fivizzano led the service.

In a closing homage to the deceased, a man intoned one of *il professore*'s poems. I'd always liked listening to Bononi recite his work, but in that ill-lit, chilly cathedral, the lines sounded bombastic. Closing my eyes, I heard Bononi himself contemplating the end of his contest with life: *and only one of us will win.*

When I call my mother a few days later, to update her on the situation at the castle—Raffaella is struggling in the aftermath of Bononi's death—Mom receives the news with her usual sangfroid. Then one of her hearing aids whistles, and she asks me to hold on so she can adjust it.

I'm back, she says after a moment. And I've put my tape player on the floor—maybe that'll help with the feedback . . .

What are you reading, I ask after she stops fiddling with the aid, finally silencing its shrill cries.

Well, I've almost finished a pretty good mystery. By the way, how do you say *books* in Italian?

Libri, I answer.

I'm thinking of rereading your friend Nuala's book, Mom continues. Remind me again of its title?

Are You Somebody? I answer, returning mentally to the first time I read that memoir. How heart-throttling its honesty . . . I'd never come across an account of an Irish life—of any life—offered in language like Nuala O'Faolain's. Excoriating, celebrating, vivisecting, mourning: she did it all. Both as a writer and as a woman, Nuala was formidable; no one ever got a curveball past her, as my father would say.

It was my mother who first told me about *Are You Somebody?*, back in the late 1990s; she'd heard about it on the radio.

Trust me, she said, you've really got to read this one. Introduced
by a mutual friend, Nuala and I first met in Brooklyn in 2003,
and quickly grew close. As it happened, she lived a couple of
blocks from me, so we saw one another a few times each month.
We had a favorite spot for brekkers, as she called it: eggs, bacon,
coffee for her, tea for me. An astonishing talker, Nuala bristled
with intelligence, humor, scorn, longing, and pain. No subject
was off-limits, but she loathed chitchat. I'd enter our breakfast
joint and scan it for her blonde head; Nuala would be seated
in "our" booth, reading the paper, readying to lob earfuls of
opinion at me. Politics enraged and galvanized her; literature
was sustenance. She was wonderfully well-read. During each
breakfast, our emotional lives would be subjected to intense
examination—exhausting, exhilarating.

I'm healthy as a trout, she told me in passing in 2008, a week
or so after complaining of a leg that felt oddly heavy—*I just don't
know what this feckin' leg-dragging is all about*... That was shortly
before a young intern in a New York hospital emergency room
announced, rather as if he were letting her know she had the flu,
that there was a tumor in her brain. She died a few months later,
at sixty-seven.

Yes, Mom responds, breaking into my reverie. Yes—I'd like
to read that book again. It was so good. Can you order it for me?

Sure, I say. Anything else you want?

I'm getting tired of thrillers. I'd like something big, a
nice long novel I've never read before. How about *Crime and
Punishment*?

Yikes, Mom, I answer. Now there's an undertaking.... I'll try to get you the translation by Pevear and Volokhonsky.

Whatever you think's best, my mother says.

After our conversation ends, I look for my copy of *Crime and Punishment* on the bookshelf in the living room, then realize it's in Brooklyn.

I locate the novel's first chapter online and reread the opening, that moment when Raskolnikov, the murderer-to-be, asks himself what people are most afraid of. His answer is chillingly simple, and just as chillingly complex. *A new step, their own new word*, Raskolnikov asserts. And what a step *he* takes!

I'm sure my mother will respond to the book, but it may keep her awake more than she'd like. Though I haven't reread the novel in ages, I recall how much its protagonist's eerie clarity spooked me. Smart, unreliable, utterly mixed-up—his name suggests the Russian word for *split*—Raskolnikov is nonetheless sure of himself. How could that be possible, I recall wondering when I first read the book. To be so regularly self-confident and such a god-awful mess at the same time? A quick search online for quotes from the novel yields one answer: ... *in the midst of my laughing I'd give way to sadness, fall into ludicrous despondency and once again start the whole process all over again ... round and round like a squirrel on a wheel.*

Then I replay in my mind the close of my conversation with Mom. You'd better read the novel, too, she said. I did once, Mom, I replied. But I should reread it. Problem is, I've got stuff I'm teaching, plus there's always other stuff my students tell me about . . . It's endless—I'm forever falling behind.

Well, read this book, my mother ordered sternly. Because I'll need to talk to you about it.

To everyone's surprise, we get snow in Castiglione in February.

Raffaella and her dog romp in it, and I'm relieved to see her laughing for the first time in months. We make snow angels in the midday glare. Raffaella bakes one of her chocolate cakes, and we have big slices of it with hot strong coffee in her kitchen.

She's awaiting Bononi's ashes, which his brother obdurately refuses to bring to the castle. They're at war, Raffaella and the Bononi family, over the question of how to deal with *il professore*'s remains. Bononi wanted nothing to do with marble headstones. His wishes (written out in his shaky hand, shortly before his demise) were that he be interred below the castle's tower, in the upper part of the garden. His brother has interpreted his words to mean that the ashes should go inside the tower, in an urn—not outside, in the earth. Since no agreement has been reached, the ashes remain with the brother.

Antonio and I go to Switzerland for several weeks at the start of March. We're in residence at Looren House, an international center for translation.

I've never worn sunglasses in winter, but I do in Switzerland; the snow's dazzle is near-blinding. We're snow-surrounded, snow-dominated. We take afternoon walks in the stuff; it's deep but surprisingly powdery. In the evenings, after hard work and the nice fatigue of our snow walks, we make dinner and drink red wine with the other translators at Looren House. If no common language exists—and some evenings it doesn't—we talk collectively around our mutual-comprehension difficulties, triangulating among English, German, French, Italian, Hungarian, and Dutch.

A poet who writes in Romansch arrives for a day; we all listen to him read with his Dutch translator. The two of them sound like strange birds, chippering and swooping. I don't need to understand a word to know I like the poems a lot.

Have you finished *Crime and Punishment*, I ask my mother when I call her in mid-March after our return from Switzerland.

Almost, she says. It's great! I've had to take it slow, but it's been so worth it—such a wonderful book. How far are along are you? When can we talk about it?

Oh, Mom, I say, I haven't even started . . .

You haven't? she says. Yes, I know, you're translating. Well, get going—I don't have all the time in the world.

I say nothing to that. There's nothing to be said.

You know, Mom adds, the only reason I'll excuse you is that you're supposedly working on your own writing, in addition to the translation. Have you finished the draft of your novel yet?

Ma . . .

Oh, all right, she says in that larky tone she's always done to perfection: half remonstrance, half indulgence. As if to say, how *do* I put up with you? As if to say, I *do* put up with you, you know. But you're dawdling.

She doesn't push further, yet I sense the subtext: she's impatient with me. *I'm* impatient with me, too. At this juncture it's tricky telling the difference.

We shift subjects. My mother goes into detail about my father's recent visit to the doctor (he has, it seems, a heart-related ailment of his own, though not as serious as hers), and I find myself tuning out, summoning to mind various book titles I've urged on her in the past. Some she's liked a lot, others not as much, a few not in the least.

She responded very strongly to Julia Glass's debut novel, *Three Junes*. I've yet to read it, though Mom's pushed me to. I'm balky about some of her suggestions, aware of the double standard I'm imposing; my mother is invariably open to my urgings. In this realm I like to feel independent, not an obedient daughter but recalcitrant, even rebellious. I fear I'll dislike a book she admires, and then I won't hear the end of it. Truth is, my reading life has never been very susceptible to other people's urgings. This isn't normally an issue between my mother and me, but in recent years she's been keen for us to read certain titles together, and I've resisted.

We've managed nonetheless. She loved Sándor Márai's *Embers*; its careful unpacking of a friendship appealed to her. And we both liked a novel by Peter Høeg, *Smilla's Sense of Snow*, for its strangeness of setting and action. She was impressed by several stories of Edna O'Brien and William Trevor that I pressed her to read. Milan Kundera, however, left her cold, as did Italo Calvino—a disappointment to me, as they're among my favorite authors.

Like her, I've learned not to press too hard. Our shared love of reading is the main thing. One of my greatest quiet pleasures is watching my mother with her audio player in her lap, listening deeply to a book. And one of hers is hearing her adult children read aloud to her; when we do, her face softens in contentment.

Is she recalling, I wonder, those few years when, still sighted, she could read to her very young kids? I have no clear memory of this, though it must've occurred. That experience is inscribed on the wax tablets of our minds, as Socrates described memory. Some of it is blurred by now, perhaps. But Mom was trained by Braille to read even the lightest of markings, the faintest trails; I expect she can make out what I cannot.

Finished with her medical update, Mom returns unexpectedly to the subject of books.

I reread your first novel a few weeks ago, she says.

Startled, I say nothing at first, my chest tightening with unexpected fear. Am I afraid she's read the novel again because something about it dissatisfied or baffled her the first time? Or that she liked it then, and wants to refresh her memory before leaving it behind for good?

Why, Mom? I ask.

Oh, I don't know, I just felt I . . . I wanted to reread it, that's all. And I liked it just as much the second time around.

As quickly as she's introduced it, she changes the subject. Has she sensed my discomfort, or is she dodging her own? We chat briefly about my father's forgetfulness (he claims, Mom reports, that he's got CRS disease—Can't Remember Shit), and then the call's over.

I pull on my sneakers for a walk to Croce so I can gaze at the *borgo* from across the way. The midafternoon air is crisp; I gulp it down. Tristana follows me, then stops when we near *la colla*. The most dog-like cat in Castiglione, she's clear about her loyalty's limits. With one agile leap she's on the wall, then over it and into the underbrush, off to her own investigations.

I walk uphill. At the old chapel of L'Annunziata, a nicely restored inn up the road, I slow down to catch my breath.

I'm hearing my mother's voice in my head. Not words; just tones, the music of it. As if she's singing me into courage and calm. Anxiety is time's useless cloak, she's singing. And death's trying to strip me of it. I should in any case let it go.

I stop walking, close my eyes, and inhale. An image arrives of the floor in that cool, dim room in Carrara where Bononi's body was laid out for viewing. The marble so soft-looking, as though he and the rest of us could sink into it. The floor might've been a cloud that had drifted down our way, settling beneath our feet.

12. Listening in the Dark

CASTIGLIONE IS PROFOUNDLY QUIET. ALSO SURPRISINGLY noisy.

A few weeks during each summer, the itinerant priest who serves our part of Lunigiana comes to the little church up by the castle. The click of his heels is audible as he trots along the cobblestone lane, an all-black shadow in a hurry—he's always late for Mass . . . After services, the bell in the castle's tower rings; across the valley, another answers from the church in Virgoletta. (The two villages' bells aren't synchronized, so the hours get sounded twice, a few minutes apart; I never know which is the right time.) Intermittently, a couple of donkeys weigh in dolefully. Feral cats quarrel from time to time.

So the silence does get broken. But there are not many human voices, rarely any mechanical noises, and no music save that of birdsong. Which isn't to say Castiglione's gloomy; the vistas are too broad for that. And a hum of energy is palpable here, even after the sun goes down. From the woods come occasional warnings, jeerings, protests; now and then an outright shriek, the kind that stops a person's blood.

Mostly, though, the nights are void of sound. And of light, too. Unless the moon is out, the sky is a jeweler's pitch-black velvet cloth sprinkled with diamonds. The *borgo*'s wrought-iron streetlamps (few in number, all dim) do nothing to dull the sparkle. Neck craned to take it all in, a little dizzy, I feel sometimes I'll fall upward into it.

What's ineffable in Castiglione—the traumas and scars of history, the seasons' rigors and reliefs—stirs each individual consciousness like some invisible spoon. There are few of us here, but our collective seeping-forth of experience and feeling is without pause; the brew thickens.

We're all mindful of living in a near-deserted space. There's no longer a powerful *capitano* in residence in the castle, as during the fifteenth and sixteenth centuries. There are no more Florentine noble families in the palazzi below the church, no more peasants in the stone houses flanking the *borgo*'s main lane, no more soon-to-be emigrants to L'America, no more Partisan sympathizers, no more postwar returnees. Nor any current dwellers under the age of fifty.

If during an afternoon walk I encounter one of my neighbors, I can sense in his or her expression some perception starting to stretch like a cat after a nap. Or some strong emotion contracting into a tight hard knot, some inchoate longing about to emerge. My neighbor can sense, I'm sure, the same things in me. But nothing's said of any of this; we speak instead of weather or food. We haven't words for this stirring within us, or for how we've each been spending at least a little of our time since we last met: with the dead, who regale us with tales we fear we'll forget, or distort in the retelling.

An owl sometimes breaks the quiet. How to feel when it addresses us so eerily, comically, menacingly, sorrowfully?

I once heard the Emerson String Quartet play the last quartet of Shostakovich's cycle. Before the music began, the hall's lights were turned off. The four musicians sat at a distance from one another, not in their usual cluster, and proceeded to play in pitch-blackness.

It's a slow-moving piece, that fifteenth. Adagio all the way. Slow, yet beautifully taut. On the score, the composer wrote instructions for the first movement: "Play [it] so that flies drop dead in mid-air and the audience leaves the hall in sheer boredom." That evening, however, as the first haunting notes emerged out of nowhere and the quartet commenced its tense journey from agita to acceptance, no one in the audience was bored. We were all balanced on a razor's edge between exhilaration and dismay, our collective breath held.

In Castiglione's castle, among the hundreds of books, manuscripts, and incunabula stuffed into various armoires—even in the cellars—are first editions of Dante in multiple languages, a *Divine Comedy* printed in 1472, original works by Petrarch, and letters of Leopardi and other writers. The contents of Loris Jacopo Bononi's library would slacken the jaws of any seasoned archivist. Bononi also collected musical instruments, paintings, sculpture, furniture, and household objects, all dating from the fifteenth through the eighteenth centuries.

Structurally, the castle is just as it was during its heyday. A few frescoes are missing, and the kitchen and baths have been modernized; otherwise, all's the same. Entering, you feel as if you've just taken a long fall backward in time, clunked your head, then woken up, dazed but unhurt—indeed, dazzled—to find you're no longer in the early twenty-first century but in the middle of the Renaissance. Lining the walls of the castle's huge entry hall are portraits of various dead people, all connected in some way with Lungianese history. Their sober faces peer down from the walls of the music room and library as well.

Tucked in various corners are small photographs of Bononi and Raffaella. In these photos *il professore* wears his usual hawkeyed expression, while Raffaella grins engagingly at the camera. Why such small images of Loris and Raffaella, I remember wondering when I first took note of the photos. Aren't *their* lives worth celebrating, too, especially since they've done the heavy lifting around here? Or will nicely framed photos come only with their deaths? Is that what it takes to merit attention in this place?

A few weeks before Bononi's passing, Raffaella made tea for Antonio and me. As we'd done on other occasions, we talked with her and *il professore* about the castle's future. It was drizzling outside, the late-October afternoon unusually cool. We all sat by the large fireplace off the kitchen.

Bononi was ill and weak but voluble. He'd sunk his fortune into this place, and some deep-pocketed person or entity would need to step in and take over its cultivation after his death. Who, when, how? He and Raffaella had not managed to come up with a clear answer to these questions. As he talked, his body seemed to hum with agitation.

You've given so much energy to this, said Antonio.

My life, said Bononi.

Wincing a bit, he shifted in his chair.

I live here, and I write, he added. To myself. To my unknown life. I'll never know her, always long for her, she'll always be a stranger to me . . . I came to Castiglione del Terziere to build this castle idea, and to write. It's what I was meant to do. The rest was a preface.

Loris, said Raffaella, take your heart medicine now, please.

Che balle! Always handing me pills!

He smiled at her, tenderly.

Raffaella threw another couple of logs on the fireplace, jabbing them expertly with an antique poker. Alarmed by the noise, one of the castle's newest kittens, no more than six weeks old, hopped onto Bononi's lap. He lifted it up and thrust it like a handkerchief into a front patch-pocket in his wool jacket. The kitten's tiny head and paws emerged, but it didn't wiggle further out. Bononi massaged the animal's fuzzy crown with a crooked forefinger. Both of them—man and cat—gazed at us, their eyes an identical china-blue color.

Drink your water, added Raffaella. Wash those pills down.

Doctors! said *il professore*, his grin partly a grimace. *Tutti matti*—they're all crazy! *Credetemi*, I know what I'm talking about.

He tossed back his handful of pills with a gulp. The kitten slipped from his pocket and vanished into the kitchen.

Listen, Bononi continued, his tone urgent now. These books in my library, I've told you already, they all found *me*, not the other way around. It happened because it was meant to happen. I've always been loyal to Lunigiana; my loyalty brought me here. These books followed me, tracked me down, they tell me things . . . it's not just the words. And something will happen to protect them. I am sure of this.

Raffaella poured us more tea. I leaned forward, not because I couldn't hear Bononi but because whenever *il professore* spoke about his library, articulating a lifetime of desire, I found myself wanting to get closer to such strangeness. What sort of person amassed a library in a castle? This *biblioteca* wasn't merely a storage center. For Bononi it was a repository of esoteric insights—emotional, intellectual, spiritual—which he'd alchemized into poems. He was proud, to be sure, of the physical beauty of his old volumes, especially those bound in hand-tooled leather, their covers and spines stamped in gold. Yet Bononi's library wasn't meant to be impressive in that way. What's more, it was organized and displayed so haphazardly that no visitor could appreciate what it actually contained. A serious archivist or book conservationist would be appalled by

Bononi's collection—not that *il professore* cared; he scorned such people.

I want anyone to be able to touch all these books and manuscripts, he said. They *have* to touch them. That's how my library will keep living.

Finishing our tea, Antonio and I stood and pulled on our coats; it was time to leave. We said goodbye to Bononi, who ordered us not to forget our umbrellas. Raffaella and Mia accompanied us down the wide steps to the lower terrace; despite the rain, Mia's tail wagged as we headed to the huge iron gate at the base of the ramp.

No, *amore*, said Raffaella to her dog, restraining Mia. You can't go find Pedro now. He's at home, keeping dry. *Ciao!* she called to Antonio and me, waving as the gate clanged shut behind us.

We headed down the path to our house, raindrops tinkling all around. Visualizing Bononi's bookshelves, I realized they reminded me of the shelves of a smart but sloppy child. Their seeming disarray reflected the movements of a mind incessantly noting links and intersections, seeking coherence. During our tea, Bononi had told us that his *biblioteca* gave him access to an interior space, a realm of truths at once hidden and open, available to all. What he hadn't said, though I was certain he felt it, was that this realm belonged to the dead, could belong to no one else. They and not he were its real curators.

* * *

A few months earlier, we'd joined Bononi in the *sala grande* for one of his castle tours. Antonio reminded me about that afternoon as we shook our wet umbrellas over the doormat before entering our house.

Il professore always used to begin his tours in the castle's main hall. All manner of people came to visit the castle each week—not in droves, to be sure, yet a reliable flow: tourists, local teachers and schoolkids, members of historical societies, the occasional journalist or local politician. One never knew who might walk up the hill. Having done a tour myself during our initial visit to the village, I could still recall shaking Bononi's hand for the first time. He'd worn a beautiful linen shirt and pants, and flashed his winning grin. We'd listened to him for the better part of three hours straight. *Ci ha preso quasi in ostaggio*, Antonio'd murmured after that inaugural encounter—the guy practically took us hostage, didn't he? What a talker!

On the warm August day that Antonio summoned to memory, Bononi had hosted a group of high-schoolers. We'd asked Raffaella if we could tag along. (*Certo*, she'd said—you'll get to watch him seduce them . . .) After assembling the kids and their teacher, Bononi explained how he'd restored the castle. Then he conducted a reasonably brisk run-through of the main rooms. He was clearly tired; his breath was labored. But he grinned and joked his way through the tour, and after opening a huge armoire in his study, he let all the students put their hands on a school primer dating from the fifteenth century. Look, he said, flipping to the back of the primer, here's where the kid who owned this book scribbled and drew pictures in the back—just like you guys do in your own books!

Back in the main hall, sunlight slanted through the high, lead-paned windows. The group reassembled for a final peroration from *il professore*. Two cats slunk in just as he began to talk, their bellies low to the ground as they aimed for the kitchen. Bononi paused and laughed, watching a girl try but fail to catch one of the cats. *Lascia perdere*, he told her; forget it, you can't win that game!

Then he urged the students to be proud of Lunigiana. It's yours, he said, all yours, so love it! He recited a few of his poems, gesturing extravagantly with his delicate-fingered hands; to my surprise, the students stayed quiet while he performed. When he'd finished, Bononi spent a few more minutes flirting mercilessly with the girls and using vulgar language with the boys. Then he sat, exhausted, and drank the glass of water Raffaella handed him.

The kids were won over. To me it seemed they'd sensed this was a place with a secret life. And as they listened to Bononi's accounts of the past—how a particular book had wended its way to his library, how the year 1929 (that of his birth) had been carved into the base of the castle's bell tower by some unknown laborer, how the wife of Ugolino, the child-eater in the *Inferno*, is buried under the well in Castiglione's *piazzetta*—the students and their teacher jumped willingly through his story-hoops, ready to believe each tale.

* * *

Recalling that afternoon, I wondered how Bononi had managed to sustain such confidence in his castle idea. For him, the restoration of a ruin atop a hill was the launch of pure potentiality—his own most of all.

Was his belief in the rightness of his undertaking nothing but narcissism? I didn't think so. Like Walt Whitman's, it seemed derived not from egotism but from estrangement, an alienation that couldn't be remedied yet might be repurposed. *I too am not a bit tamed, I too am untranslatable*, wrote Whitman in "Song of Myself." *And what I assume you shall assume*. For those students he'd shown around the castle, it'd been thrilling to be held captive by a seeming madman raving about rare books and declaiming poetry. Yet this castle's owner wasn't actually mad. He'd simply spent longer than most people under time's circus tent, and knew when to stop talking, fall abruptly silent, and let the reverberations of earlier music—voices of people famous and infamous, celebrated and overlooked—lap around him.

Bononi was involved with several women during his life, yet death was always the most compelling of his romances.

He'd have disagreed with this statement, would say it was life he loved, as he surely did. During his final years, he worked on a poem he described as literally and deliberately endless: a letter addressed to *una sconosciuta*, the figure of an unknown woman. She is life, he said; all life, and *his* life. He could not have her, never had her, only longed for her. Lacking her, he conjured her daily in language. Each of his additions to his ever-expanding poem got dumped into a big chest in his study, where the pages accumulated. He never looked at them, never revised what he wrote, never returned to what he'd already composed.

What he insisted upon, as he penned this extravagant work, was ongoingness: a continuous emission of words, a constant search for new ways to speak to his beloved. And what made this effort remarkable was his recognition that he and she were locked not in an embrace but in a contest:

To me it always seemed the world
was mine
and I
was jealous of my self
then
life
started seizing my world
and thus I understood
it wasn't mine
and life and I
would have to test each other
and only one of us
would win

She'll win
I'll have loved her
so much
sometimes without knowing it

* * *

After crossing the border into his eighties, Bononi rarely left the castle. Very hard of hearing, he had difficulty conducting a regular conversation. Yet he could tell stories for hours on end.

His mother figured indirectly in all of them. When he was a young boy, she told him he was exceptional; then she detached herself from him, insisting he go forth unaided, on his own. He was sent to boarding school and university. And then his mother died—leaving him imaginatively primed to re-create with other women a story of love and respect vying ceaselessly with frustration and despair.

In his twenties he became involved with a woman who, in his description, seems to have been quite like his mother: affirmative on the surface, yet wholly unavailable. (Also, he claimed, she was in love with her father.) This woman hailed, like him, from Fivizzano, though they ended up in Rome, where—by this time married—they consorted with actors, dancers, and movie folk, and café-hopped with Federico Fellini.

The public man wore silk suits and had affairs, but the private man suffered. Bononi asserted he never had any physical relationship with his wife, whom he left after ten years without divorcing her. He rarely saw or communicated with her again, yet they remained legally married till his death, Raffaella notwithstanding—consenting, in fact, to this arrangement, for reasons as complex and, to the outsider, as impenetrable as *il professore*'s own.

After leaving his wife, Bononi commenced a series of romantic entanglements, some highly dramatic. To Antonio and myself—and to numerous others, for he was anything but inhibited in detailing his personal life—Bononi spoke of lovers of his who'd killed themselves (one self-immolated, he claimed, and the other jumped off a bridge); of an affair with a woman who, he said, he then discovered was his child; of prostitutes who were his greatest teachers, not of sex but of self-affirmation.

A serving of virgin-whore tropes with a big dollop of incest and suicide on top? So it might seem; yet Bononi was too aware of his own manipulations, too invested in mythmaking as an art, to be so reductive. He followed Emily Dickinson's injunction—*tell all the truth but tell it slant*—and allowed invention to mingle freely with projection and repression in his creation of a narrative for his life. No doubt he'd have concurred with the lead character in John Dryden's comic play *Amphitryon*—"I never saw any good that came of telling truth"—although *il professore* claimed never to have told a lie, and to have paid dearly for his honesty. He might as easily have said that the words *lying* and *honesty* meant what they needed to mean to him—which is not to suggest the man was a charlatan. He was, rather, a person who found the border between fantasy and reality porous and easily traversed, and liked it that way.

What riveted me when in Bononi's presence was the struggle I felt him waging with himself, a battle requiring all his force.

His castle and its contents possessed him, not the other way around. They were at once alive and dead, which is how he saw himself as an old man. He wanted to die, he insisted—it was time to go—yet he clung to his home, his work, his sense of mission. *I was raised by my mother to be a prince*, he asserted repeatedly. Bononi wasn't speaking as a snob; he was incapable of an aristocrat's emotional detachment. What he meant was this: I was raised to believe wholly and blindly in myself, and I'm having trouble doing so, for I've become old and impotent, and my psychic and physical sufferings seem daily to outdo my strength.

In the weeks before his death, he spoke agitatedly about a demon whose existence he'd always been aware of, but whom till now he'd managed to keep at bay. One afternoon he spoke of terror lasting for hours as his mind, normally lucid, slipped and skidded . . . *I no longer knew who I was, I was someone else.* This demon of his had no physical reality; it was invisible, like toxic air.

And like anxiety, I thought. Like my own demon—which isn't, like Bononi's, intent on making me question my identity, but rather on making me second-guess and doubt myself.

What might I learn about demons from this dying man? I wasn't sure, but was struck by the fact that while describing his own, Bononi's language grew richer and stranger than usual. Reviling his enemy, he was also reveling in depicting it.

During those final days, Bononi oscillated between tenderness and cruelty toward the woman who'd been at his side for several decades, telling her in one moment that he needed her help to live and then, a minute later, that she ought to help him kill himself and was monstrous for not doing so. Where, he raged, had she hidden the kitchen knives?

That pattern of supplication and excoriation wouldn't change. Nor, before dying, would Bononi recover from the wound his mother remained for him. Why should he, a physician, have sought to heal himself at the end, since the damage had been so fruitful, had allowed so much poetry to spill forth?

My heart, he wrote in one poem, *is a wounded migrant . . . The journey a love without end.*

Now, as during the final months of *il professore*'s life, I'm writing in the garret of our old stone house. This house never belonged to a nobleman, never served as a seat of power; it lodged peasants. From its terrace I can't see the whole Magra Valley spread out before me. Nor have I spent decades contemplating this region and its history.

And that's not all. I couldn't then and can't now imagine composing an unending poem. Am tempted to say, I don't have time for that. Stories, novels, plays, poems—they have beginnings and endings. (Though not really: they are written, read, and rewritten in their readers' minds. A cycle, a continuous stirring.) And a writer makes, steals, or borrows time just like everybody else.

Compared to Bononi's, my library in Brooklyn is meager. But the books' reverberations—how I felt as and after I read that one, that one, that one . . .

When I was young, I used to lie in my bedroom at night and picture all the books on the shelves at the foot of my bed. They'd be talking with one another.

The musicians who performed Shostakovich's quartet didn't need to see one another. Their instruments' voices spoke with shattering clarity in the dark.

Sometimes I picture *il professore* gazing out his window in the middle of the night. (He was an owl who slept little, just a few hours between four and seven in the morning.) He'd be staring at the ebony sky. At stars whose explosions we're only now able to perceive, illuminations resulting from galactic blasts that have taken so long to reach us, signaling something as yet indecipherable. He'd be thinking: *the books in my library are like those stars.*

Once Bononi died, I couldn't put off confronting the question of ambition. His singular experience threw it into sharp relief, but it was bound to arise in any case.

For so long I've been earnestly marching, urged on by an inner bandmaster wielding his baton as mirthlessly as a martinet with a whip. Till now I've imagined myself reaping a bigger crop; not just publishing more, but writing something that would have to be reckoned with, a game-changer. As I picture Bononi in his study, each day penning his endless poem to his beloved, I'm struck by how he skirted the problem of ambition: by refusing any limits. He would continue that poem till he dropped, and no one could tell him otherwise, or accuse him of wasting time. While he always hoped for greater fame (and notoriety) than he received, his expressive freedom counted more. His work would eventually make its way into the right hands, in any case: of this he was ever confident.

Many are the letters the man has written his Unknown and we have read some at random, / leaving the rest to more diligent readers.

One evening shortly before her death, my friend Andrea began talking to me about her life. On this topic we'd shared a dialogue of thirty years' duration, but now both the tone and the terms were different.

She spoke with quiet sadness about the fact that she hadn't accomplished anything in the realm of art, as she'd always felt she ought to. Having studied drawing for a time at the Art Students League, she hadn't gone any further—hadn't put all her self into it, hadn't taken the leap. But that was all right, she concluded. It was enough to think of her life as her artwork. To have committed wholeheartedly to the living of it.

There's nothing greater, I reassured her when she'd finished speaking. Nothing more intrinsically valuable than that.

Yet I did have talent as an artist, she said. And I failed to fulfill it. For all kinds of reasons I didn't do what I thought I could do, should do. What I'd always hoped to do.

In the silence that followed, Andrea's gaze went limpid. Then she added—still quietly, for she was never a drama queen—that the sorrow of leaving so soon was beyond any words.

I held her hands, her wrists like twigs. Then hugged her. She seemed a bird on a branch, about to take off. The weight of speech no longer upon her, she was able to hear—as I in that moment could not—the music in the dark.

As I walked home after that conversation with her (which took place in November—I remember it was cold outside, I kept having to wipe my eyes so I could see where I was going, and at one point I broke into a run so the tears, pushed by the wind, would roll to the sides instead of fuzzing my vision), I replayed in my mind scene after scene of Andrea doing various things. Cooking, reading, dancing, watering plants, folding laundry, stacking books on a shelf, playing with her cats, talking on the phone . . . all the so-called trivialities.

Then I thought about how much I'd learned from her simply by observing her going about the business of her living. Doing all that *nothing*, the stuff we're taught to dismiss. Did it flatten her sometimes, the why-bother feeling? No doubt. But she was in natural possession of a sense of proportion, which got her over the hump. That, and her sense of humor. And when she became sick and then sicker, she was most of the time a saint about it, and for the most part without self-recrimination.

Andrea had been robbed of time; it got yanked out from under her. Yet a seemingly endless bolt of time still unfurled before *me*. I'd pulled the charm out of the Cracker Jack box; she'd drawn a skeleton from the pack of tarot cards.

Making me feel guilty about this would've been the furthest thing from Andrea's mind. It was I, not she, who silently flogged that horse. Yet even as Andrea sought to affirm that since she'd lived openheartedly she could die feeling more fulfilled—more whole—than if she'd been an artist but lived incompletely, I heard the fatigue in her tone. It was profound, caused not just by illness but by the burden that time had handed her. *You're not doing enough*, the clock's tick says. Or: *What you're doing counts for so little in the end.*

I sometimes hear Andrea's voice. Pipe down, she gripes mock-seriously. Don't you know your thoughts are a broken record?

Inside the tent we think we're listening to the dead, but it's our voices we hear, mimicking theirs. We ventriloquize, hoping thus to revive those we've lost, or perhaps merely revive ourselves. Especially when in the slough of despond, as it used to be called. *I had not thought death had undone so many*, said Dante, astonished, to Virgil. Well, yeah: it sure did, it sure does. But who are the many undone—the dead or we who still live? And how to undo the undoing?

An evening thunderstorm in Castiglione. Heavy rain on the roof.

Under the eaves of my studio, I hear the steady thrum. Looking out the window, I see the castle garden's wall—ivy-plaited in parts, mossy everywhere, water sluicing down it and down the alley and down to *la colla* and down the macadam road, to the creek that leads to the stream in Villafranca that leads to the Magra River running between Villafranca and Aulla and thence, a hour or so from here, to Bocca di Magra, the river's end, debouching into the Mediterranean.

The water says what the dead don't have time or heart to say, or what they feel they've said already. Read what's already been written, they say. Read the poems, stories, novels, essays, plays. Read the words for the first time, or again; it doesn't matter which. In any case you'll be writing them again, each time you read them—rewriting the words for yourselves. Because what you claim to hear, when you come here to listen to our voices, is only and always yourselves.

It's grown very dark; the storm has blotted out the stars. I can see nothing beyond what the dim lamp at the foot of the alley illumines.

Water in sheets now, and long rolls of thunder. Like listening to Shostakovich's Fifteenth: consoling and terrifying at once.

Up at the castle, a month before his death—still able to spend a bit of time in his study, writing to his beloved—*il professore* would have been gazing out his window during such a tempest. Hungry, always, for the natural world's dramas. He'd have been able to see only what the sole lamp by the castle gate might enlighten: the little church, the well in the *piazzetta*, the lights of a few houses across the valley. Otherwise, everything a blur.

But he'd be listening.

13. Mullets

Antonio and I are in Porto Venere, a small town on the extreme southern promontory of the Cinque Terre, facing the Gulf of La Spezia. The little island of Palmaria lies humpbacked in its harbor, with Tino and Tinetto just beyond; Byron must've gazed at them when he visited. (He swam from here to Lerici, or so the story goes.)

In summer Porto Venere gets crowded, but nobody's hanging around here on an early-April afternoon. The bar where we go after our walk is empty, its owner startled to be asked for hot tea. It isn't particularly cold outside, in fact. We've sunned ourselves on the terrace of a Gothic church that sits atop rocks at the harbor's far end, where Porto Venere juts into the sea. The little chapel is cool, gray, unperturbed. Portions of its floor date from the sixth century. Staring at the remains of what must've been a floral-inspired pattern of stone underfoot, I try imagining the individuals who'd built the church—worshippers for whom beauty was as urgent an imperative as faith. Despite everything else vying for their attention and energy, they'd found time to design a lovely floor.

Taking in the view of the Mediterranean after weeks of rain and damp in Castiglione—such a wet spring!—Antonio and I watch as a small fishing boat approaches the harbor, bucking against the waves. It goes at a good clip. Then we walk down to the docks, where the boat is doing a bit of business: some townspeople have lined up to buy fresh fish. An impromptu, pop-up *mercato* is under way.

We join the queue, surveying the *gamberoni* and *coda di rospo* and *seppie* and *naselli* and *polpi* and *cefali*. What bounty, even in wintertime! In a container at the center are a few dozen small, red-skinned, shiny fish called *triglie*.

Let's get those, says Antonio.

We bring the *triglie* home. Tristana slips in through the terrace door, enticed by the scent. We dispatch her outdoors; she sits with Big Boy, who's too scared to venture inside. Gazing hungrily through the glass door, the two cats wait while Antonio scales and guts our gift from Porto Venere.

We prepare the mullet *alla Livornese* (tomatoes, olives, capers, garlic, oil), give a bit to the cats, then serve the rest to ourselves, along with some rice and Swiss chard. Eating with relish, we wash the meal down with a bit of local Vermentino and sit quietly afterward, hands folded contentedly over bellies.

* * *

Beauty, I think, staring at my empty plate. Do I notice it, do I privilege it on a daily basis?

The sunset en route home was floridly pink-purple; the lichen on the steps up from the lane to our house glowed gray-green at dusk. Tristana's fur was cool and soft when I stroked her; Big Boy's was cool, too, and sleek as an otter's. The mullet tasted delicately sweet, the chard sharp, the rice nutty. The house smelled, after dinner, of those things and more: of centuries of dust and damp, the natural world's encroachments and leavings. All variously beautiful.

Yet beauty's not just that—not merely what my own or someone else's senses discern and deliver. Hard to say what else it is, though, or how best to acknowledge it. Scarf it down or set it on a pedestal? Revere it or revel in it? Talk about it or stay silent? Beauty can make me teeter precariously between plea-sure and discomfort, even terror. So what am I to do when I encounter it?

The fisherman would find such musings ridiculous; so would Tristana and Big Boy. Eat and be glad, they'd say. And be curious, sniff things out. That's how best to respond to beauty: wonder freely about it, go where guesswork leads. To confu-sion as well as clarity, sorrow as well as pleasure. *What seas what shores what grey rocks . . .* Sometimes groping for it, as in fog; not knowing if it exists save in the mind, or in *a world of time beyond me*, as Eliot wrote in his strange poem "Marina." *The awakened, lips parted, the hope, the new ships . . .*

* * *

Realizing no further treats are forthcoming, the cats retire to the rooftop. A few hours later, Antonio and I head up to bed.

We decide not to hang the green curtain, leaving it on the floor of our balcony. Moonlight floods the bedroom; the sky's a steel-gray vastness. Up at the castle, Mia barks as if in conversation, though nobody responds.

Before falling asleep, I picture the chapel in Porto Venere, its floor's graceful motif still visible despite cracks and holes in the stonework. How had it survived the corrosion of the salt air? The human depredations? Then I visualize the grassy ruins of the old hospice we saw up at the Lagostrello Pass. It, too, once boasted four walls and a roof. Nothing was left now, merely a faint impression in the ground where the foundations had been. Time and people had carried off the rest.

What had the hospice's floor looked like? Was it patterned? Did the colors of its stonework graduate from light to dark gray and back again? Did children ever use it for hopscotch? Would pilgrims sometimes prostrate themselves upon it? Did soldiers drag their muddy or bloody gear across it?

I hope to see it in my dreams.

14. Anniversaries

JUNE, AND WE'VE BEEN HERE A YEAR.

Valeria died six years ago this month.

Liam killed himself two months after her death.

Andrea was diagnosed with cancer eleven years ago, and passed away four years later. In between, my friend Lucy Grealy, a talented writer, exited by way of a heroin overdose.

Richard Gilman, a beloved mentor, died almost a year after Andrea's death.

Nuala died five years ago last month. As did another friend, the poet Jason Shinder. That same month, in fact.

The writer David Markson, with whom I grew very close near the end of his life, died three years ago.

Nearly all these friends were in their fifties and sixties when they departed.

I can count as many friends' kids' births during the same stretch of years. And a marriage. Oh, and a pair of divorces.

Endings, beginnings. The words' banality.

Throughout my sabbatical, have I dwelt too much on terminations and not enough on starts? Everything in Castiglione is new to me; have I stepped up, leaned in, given all this novelty a whirl? Or have I let grief bully me? Days when I've been too empty to write, sorrow-drained, capable only of solitary walks—the natural world jostling my senses, calling me to attention, though I resist . . . Have those days been absurd? Have I wasted this gift of untrammeled time?

The question is itself a waste, of course.

Look elsewhere, I imagine Mom saying.

An orange-going-into-rose descending / circle of beauty and time.

Jason Shinder's short poem "At Sunset" equates dying with the sun's setting—a risky move, since the trope's not original. But the poem executes it beautifully. In a tone stripped of self-pity or reproach, "At Sunset" ends with this: *You have nothing to be sad about.* That circle of beauty and time, the poem says, can be perceived only by way of grief—and grief not after death but right now. And then grief, too, must be relinquished.

Jason was a colleague of mine; we both taught for many years in the Bennington Writing Seminars. He was not only a terrific poet but also a superb anthologist and tireless activist.

Jason founded the YMCA's National Writer's Voice, a lively network of literary arts centers serving tens of thousands of people nationwide. Whenever I think of my lanky friend—his humor droll, his smile a little lopsided—I think *generous*.

A beautiful dancer, Jason often moved to music with arms aloft, hips swiveling in effortless syncopation. Everyone wanted to dance with him, literally and figuratively, but Jason was challenged by desire—others' and his own. He longed for and resisted intimacy, physical and emotional. *From nothing nothing could come*, he concluded in another of his poems, "About a Man." *From nothing nothing could be taken*. Ambivalence was painful equipoise; poetry was how he broke its grip.

What more is life than to live it? he wrote to me, not long before dying of leukemia; he was fifty-three. *And living, as I understand it, if you are lucky enough, is a certain kind of attention and, if you are luckier, a window that opens now and then on a battlefield in which the armies in you no longer see each other as enemies but as children.*

My mother surely has her own anniversaries to remember. Endings, especially. Yet she rarely speaks of them. Maybe they're at once too ordinary and too numinous for her to acknowledge.

How often I've entered a room where she's sitting quietly, hands in her lap, and realized she's unaware of my presence. How often I've stood and watched her, unable to fathom what she might be experiencing in her illumined interior.

She's learned over time to be out of time, freed of it.

Whenever we give ourselves over to poems or stories, Jason wrote, *we are giving ourselves over, in part, to the interior life . . . So please let us encourage each other to go there, if for no other reason than this—to stay close to what matters most—and if such does not write the poem, it will almost always help us write the life, without which there is no poem.*

July now, and the days so long we dine on the terrace at nine-thirty. We don't need candlelight till ten; then bats swoop nearby, emboldened by the dark. Occasionally they carom through the terrace, wing-beats audible.

Porco pipistrello! says Antonio, dodging a bat one evening. Can you believe we'll be leaving here in a month?

No, I say, I can't believe it—nor that it's been more than a year since that bat flew into our bedroom . . .

A cat in *la colla* has had kittens. One of the babies' eyes are infected; Raffaella says she'll pick up some ointment to treat it.

Roberto, one of the renovators of the Madonna, gives us a couple of bottles of his olive oil as a gift. We helped him harvest the olives last fall. I have photos of him at the *frantoio,* grinning as he watches a great many little green ovals descending the shoot to the macerator. When I uncap one of the bottles, the smells of those days rush at me.

Use it up by year's end, Roberto says of the oil, or it'll turn. Store it someplace cool.

On a marble slab, maybe? I think. We've got one in our kitchen in Brooklyn. Not Carrara marble, but still, it'll do the trick.

Nonno! yells Antonio's grandson Milo as he trots up the lane. *Ho visto le capre!* He's seen the goats on the hill opposite the cemetery. All are thriving, including a new pair of brown-and-white kids. Recounting the scene, hands sketching the air, Milo prances in delight.

15. Phone Call

A WEEK BEFORE WE LEAVE CASTIGLIONE TO RETURN TO Brooklyn—seven days till the end of my *caesura*—I call my parents.

My mother picks up the phone. There is silence as I hear her fumbling, first with the receiver and then with her hearing aid, which squeaks a little. I know what she's doing: feeling with thumb and forefinger for the small toggle switch on the side of the aid she wears in her phone ear, as she calls it. She can't see the switch. She must grope for it.

Oh, she says before anything else—before *hello* or *who's calling*—oh, what's wrong with this phone . . . wait a minute . . . Yes? Who is it?

It's me, I say, your oldest. Calling you from Italy.

What? she says, and I know she can't hear.

It's me, I repeat loudly, your oldest . . . This is a little joke with us—my identifying myself to my mother in this way, quasi-bureaucratically.

Ah, she says after a moment, yes, my oldest . . . She chuckles.

I ask how she's doing.

What? she says.

I repeat myself.

Your voice isn't . . . , she begins, then stops, and I know it won't work—she won't be able to hear any more. Either the phone or her hearing aid is on the fritz. It's been like this recently; I've called a few times, we've exchanged a few words, and then she's had to end the call because some element of the technology that's supposed to serve her has failed, and she can hear nothing I've said.

She's awaiting a new pair of aids, but my father isn't optimistic they'll help with phone calls. Her hearing's better in person, he told me recently. Lousy, but better. You still have to yell at her, though, he added. When are you coming home, anyway—I've lost track of your schedule, my memory's shot, I can't keep anything straight . . .

Now I resume talking, loudly, into the phone. Mom, I say, can you hear me, Mom? How are you, and how's Dad?

I can't hear you, she says. Her tone has edged toward but doesn't tip into plaintive, because my mother doesn't do plaintive. Sounding like that offends her sense of self.

I say something else, yelling now. My mother still can't hear. She makes a slight chuffing sound into the receiver, like someone out of breath. I can sense her distress; it's water behind a dam, a lot of weight and pressure wanting to break through, but what good does a dam-break do? It just makes a mess.

I can't hear you, she says after a few more moments.

I stop yelling, because what good does yelling do? It, too, makes a mess. There's silence for a moment, as though we were two boxers in the ring, exhausted by a tough round. Then my mother speaks.

I can't hear you, so you should just hang up, she says quietly. Her tone is now poised between resignation and frustration—balanced there with such essential dignity, her refusal of bitterness or self-pity so adamant, that I cannot let my heart strangle itself (as it wishes to do, to put itself out of its misery) but instead try to chivvy it into standing straight and tall. Get up, I tell my heart, get up!

Oh, Mom . . . I can say nothing but this. Then I go silent.

My mother has, of course, not heard what I've said. But she speaks.

So what can I tell you, she says, affecting a breezy tone of voice. Well, let's see . . . I can tell you that your father's gone for the mail. I can tell you that I'm fine, and I can tell you . . . that I love you. That's all, you should get off the phone now, just hang up, okay? Because I can't hear you.

Never in my mother's life has she uttered to me the phrase *I can tell you that I love you*. On occasion she's told me she loves me, yes, but never like this—as though reporting on the weather, or offering the latest update from the assisted-living community. Behind her blitheness lies what she wants—needs—to convey, even though she's speaking into a void. Poking a stick in the eye of silence.

You'd better not blow it, I warn myself.

Inwardly I get down on my knees, knowing I must accept not just Mom's deafness, her blindness, her wheelchair-boundness, but also—most of all—her death. Though there's no actual reason to believe it's around the corner. Mom's a survivor, after all, and for the past twelve months she's been her usual wry self.

The phone line hums slightly; I wait a few beats. In telling me to hang up, it's as if my mother has just said *I'm leaving* instead of *you go now*. As though the usual directionality of things—I, her oldest, am the one who's supposed to go away, to spend a year in an Italian village while she stays on the geezer farm, as my father calls it—is now being reversed, and I must stay put while she readies to depart.

Yes, I think, of course. This reversal is what we've come to; why be startled by it?

The receiver feels clammy in my hand. It strikes me as absurd that, closing in on sixty years, I must still be learning all this, and that she, nearing ninety, must be crafty in communicating it—like the mother of a squalling toddler who gets the kid to behave without having to raise her voice . . . So careful not to complicate things, or burden me with her sorrows. And yet, needless to say, she has failed in her effort to protect me, as mothers everywhere do. Or to protect herself: did I not leave her, long ago?

Needless to say.

And so, phone receiver and its void still at my ear, I don't do as my mother has just done—speak the words *I can tell you that I love you*, hoping she'll hear them—for the simple reason that I know she won't. I do as I'm told, and hang up.

16. Coda

April 2014 in Brooklyn, windy, brisk.

The cruelest month? Perhaps, yet magnolia blossoms splash pink-purple-white against an azure sky, oblivious to the chill.

Four weeks ago, in mid-March, the forsythia began flowering in Castiglione del Terziere. Closing my eyes, I can see the moss softening on the castle garden's walls, its springtime sponginess . . . Can see crocuses in bloom, little white tassels in the grass. The rooster in *la colla* noisy once more, after winter's long silence.

Here, there: *qui, lá*. Without planning or intending to be, I find myself split. Perhaps this sensation, exhilarating and discomfiting, is simply a reflection of a deeper conundrum. *Our lives are Swiss— / So still, so cool*, wrote Emily Dickinson. *Till, some odd afternoon, / The Alps neglect their curtains, / And we look farther on . . .*

Now and then a glimpse, a longer view.

And this, from another of her poems: *Ourself, behind ourself concealed, / Should startle most . . .*

Eight months it's been since Antonio and I returned to Brooklyn after our *caesura*. Eight months!

A long time; no time at all.

Shortly before leaving Castiglione at the end of last August, we did something altogether unplanned: we bought a house in the village. It sits across from the church, on the *piazzetta* below the castle. Forlorn and neglected, its roof a leaky mess, the house was put on the market by the local Catholic diocese, which had used it as the *canonica*. No priest had lived in it for years. The diocese wished to sell the house quickly—and was willing to do so quite cheaply—in order to repair the bell tower and the church's interior. So we took the plunge.

Our neighbor Daniel, mastermind of the Madonna's renovation, offered to serve as our contractor. He introduced us to an architect, Stefano, who several years earlier had managed the restoration of L'Annunziata, the lovely inn up the hill, and who now agreed to oversee our project. After we left, Daniel and two other men got to work. They took down walls, installed anti-earthquake beams, rebuilt the top floor and terrace, and put up a new terra-cotta roof. Astonished, we opened our computers every few weeks to find photos from Daniel: here the roof, there the walls; here the earthquake beams, there the window frames. In mid-December, we were able to move in. Small things remained to be done, but the upper part of the house was essentially finished.

We passed the holidays in our new home, then went back to Brooklyn in early January to resettle into our American lives. But not for long: in March we returned to Castiglione for a few weeks, to check on the renovation of two studios on the ground floor—the *canonica*'s former donkey stables. Dark, dank, and filthy when we first saw them, these spaces were being transformed by Daniel and his two colleagues into cheerful studios.

During that March fortnight, I watched the forsythia come into bloom. Tristana materialized, letting us know she knew where we lived now, and expected to be fed. Big Boy was down in *la colla*, an infrequent but still-living presence. And I realized I'd learned to inhabit two states at once, which was how my grandmother Nell used to put it, gazing across the way at the lush trees on the Pennsylvania side of the river: *I live in two states. But I know which I'm in when I'm in it.*

My mother died in October 2013, around the time the new roof went up.

That fall, even while gazing at Daniel's photos of a house more than halfway through its renovation, I was plunging daily down the ravine of loss and crumpling into a fetal ball at the bottom. I'd told myself I had prepared for this, or at least tried to, yet I found myself paralyzed by unreadiness. Naturally I coped, if that's the right word; I'm my mother's daughter, she taught me to carry on. I did what had to be done, what would save me: my work. But there lay my heart in the deepest of ditches.

Up, I sometimes heard Mom saying. Get up.

I wondered if what my mother must have felt while pregnant, awaiting my and my siblings' arrivals—at once prepared and completely unready for us—was an emotion as intense as mine now, only in a totally different register, in another language. Perhaps both intensities are insusceptible to speech, and must be lived through in silence.

Her death from pneumonia wasn't quick or easy. Though she'd have said it could've been worse.

It happened in a fortnight. At first she was able to keep speaking, but then she was taken to the hospital, gasping for air, and her hearing aids were removed in the ambulance. It wasn't possible to replace and adjust them for her: she lacked the strength to explain their proper placement. I think she was simply finished with talking. Lying on her side in a hospital bed, pale and exhausted, she seemed impatient in the way I imagine a fetus is, for the arduous, inevitable passage to be over with.

I touched her face, stroking her forehead, hoping my hands would speak for me. When I was very young, she'd sometimes stroked the skin between my eyebrows as I lay with my head in her lap. Using her thumb, gently. You remember this even now, don't you, I begged her silently as I stroked that same spot on her face. You remember all you did, all you've done for me?

The overtakelessness of those / Who have accomplished Death: those opening lines of another Dickinson poem, brief and peculiar, come to me now.

To be *overtakeless*—what does that mean? It means you cannot be caught up with or surpassed.

Dickinson called it *majestic*, this quality. More so than any of Earth's other majesties.

Sitting at my mother's bedside hours before her death, listening to the rasp of her breathing, I recalled how, a few days before falling ill in September, she'd told me she wanted to visit Castiglione.

I'll come without your father, she'd said. He hates flying, you know. But that's all right, I can be in a wheelchair and you can travel with me. Or you could just meet me at the airport in Milan . . . I can't travel in winter, your father would worry too much. But once it's warmer—next spring—I'll visit, I'll come stay in the village. Just for a few days. I want to see it.

And here we are: April, springtime.

I'm once again back in Brooklyn—*this* home, not *that* one. And my mother's visiting Castiglione. In my mind I've brought her there.

I imagine her reactions. By now it's mild; she won't need her red wool coat. She's made her way up the hill, under the arch, past the ramp to the castle, down to the *piazzetta*. Has she seen the roses on the cistern behind our new house, or met Tristana yet? She'll find the key to the front door in the electric-meter box, and enter. What'll she think of the living-room book-shelves? Her gold necklace: will she open the top drawer of my bureau and see I've left it there?

I can only guess.

Acknowledgments

This memoir in essays started out as a journal for myself. Thanks go to Sheridan Hay for urging me to meander without purpose. For an early, abbreviated draft of the book, I received helpful editorial feedback from Barbara Graham.

Versions of several essays herein appeared in the following literary magazines: "Go Tell Your Father," *AGNI* (2012); "The Island and the Boat," *A Public Space* (2013); and "What a Circus!," *The Southampton Review* (2014). I undertook an online exchange of essays with Jennifer Acker, editor of *The Common*, in 2012–13, and elements of my *contributo* found their way into this book.

The final version would not have come to pass without the exceptional insight and astute editing of Leigh Newman. I am indebted to her, and grateful to the entire Catapult team for their enthusiastic support, professionalism, and kindness.

To my neighbors in Castiglione del Terziere, in particular *la famiglia* Muntean and Raffaella Paoletti, *grazie di cuore*.

And above all to Antonio Romani, my beloved, *sine qua non*.

Valeria Genzini, Richard Gilman, Lucy Grealy, David Markson, Andrea Massey, Nuala O'Faolain, Liam Rector, and Jason Shinder: I was and am blessed by these friends' inestimable gifts of themselves. This offering is in their memory.

About the Author

Martha Cooley is the author of the national bestseller *The Archivist*, a *New York Times* Notable Book and New and Noteworthy paperback, and *Thirty-Three Swoons*. Her first novel was published in a dozen foreign markets. Cooley's short fiction and essays have appeared in *A Public Space*, *AGNI*, *The Southampton Review*, *The Common*, *PEN America*, *Washington Square*, and elsewhere. She has served as a contributing editor at *The Writer's Chronicle* and is currently a contributing editor at *A Public Space*. Her co-translations of Italian fiction and poetry include Antonio Tabucchi's story collection *Time Ages in a Hurry* and a selection of contemporary poetry in *Those Who from Afar Look Like Flies: The Novecento, Part 3* (forthcoming from University of Toronto Press). A professor of English at Adelphi University, Cooley taught for fifteen years in the Bennington Writing Seminars. She divides her time between Queens, New York, and Castiglione del Terziere, Italy. She is married to the writer and translator Antonio Romani. Their American cat, Zora, is named after one of the cities in Italo Calvino's *Invisible Cities*, and their Italian cat, Tristana, is named after the medieval knight.